Most Americans believe that a university is a place where professors teach students. They are wrong. **THE CLOSED CORPORATION** cites names, facts and figures to document a quite different picture——the university as an industrial community, run by teams of management executives, staffed by a faculty group eager to sell their services to private enterprise or government, and dependent on older graduate students as a pool of cheap labor.

The general citizenry may be surprised to learn that one of the reasons they pay high prices for medicine is because the universities ganged together and lobbied Congress in behalf of the drugs companies; that the professor of medieval history at Princeton University runs from his classes to the Central Intelligence Agency, where he helps straighten out spies; and that Yale University hawks about a mutual fund.

THE CLOSED CORPORATION probes the self-perpetuating authority of trustees and administrators, the private back-room deals, the power moves and the hidden subsidies that make our major universities "the largest secret organizations within the nation."

"... a powerful indictment, bristling with names and facts. This book may well become a handbook for student protesters."
 —*New York Times Book Review*

MORE BALLANTINE BOOKS
YOU WILL ENJOY

THE CLOSED
CORPORATION

AMERICAN
UNIVERSITIES
IN CRISIS

James Ridgeway

BALLANTINE BOOKS   •   NEW YORK

ACKNOWLEDGMENTS

Several people assisted me in making inquiries. I am especially grateful to Frances Lang. Robert Kaufman, John M. Nicholl, Robin Reisig, Robert Wells and Carol Williams did some of the more intricate background reporting. Others who worked on the project include: Eric Chester, Stephen Cox, Stephen Leberstein, Peter Orris, Susan Pralgever, Roger Rapoport, Rina Rosenberg, Curtis Seltzer, Paula Stern and Anne Sutherland. Ann Tillman typed the manuscript. Gilbert Harrison, editor of the *New Republic,* kindly granted me leave of absence to work on the book. My father gave me a sound idea of what an education could be. I am, of course, responsible for all the information in the book; the opinions set forth are mine, and do not necessarily represent those of any of the above.

J. R.

FOR PAT

Contents

"Of course, when all is said, it is not learn-ing but the spirit of service that will give a college place in the public annals of the na-tion. It is indispensable, it seems to me, if it is to do its right service, that the air of affairs should be admitted to all its classrooms. I do not mean the air of party politics, but the air of the world's transactions, the consciousness of the solidarity of the race, the sense of the duty of man toward man, of the presence of men in every problem, of the significance of truth for guidance as well as for knowledge, of the potency of ideas, of the promise and the hope that shine in the face of all knowledge. There is laid upon us the compulsion of the national life. We dare not keep aloof and closet ourselves while a nation comes to its maturity. The days of glad expansion are gone, our life grows tense and difficult; our re-source for the future lies in careful thought, providence, and a wise economy; and the school must be of the nation."

—*Woodrow Wilson*

1. The Machine

"The function of college is not to prepare you for life," the philosopher Paul Weiss said. "It is to prepare you to be a man, and when you are a man you can face life, whatever the conditions."

In all likelihood most Americans believe, like Weiss, that universities are places where professors teach students. They are wrong. In fact, the university looks more like a center for industrial activity than a community of scholars.

The general citizenry may be surprised to learn that they pay such high prices for medicines partly because the universities ganged together and lobbied Congress in behalf of the drug companies; that the professor of medieval history at Princeton University runs from his classes to the Central Intelligence Agency, where he helps straighten out the spies; and that Yale University hawks about a mutual fund.

In the *Notes on the Post Industrial State,* Daniel Bell makes it plain enough: "The university, which is the place where theoretical knowledge is sought, tested and codified in a disinterested way, becomes the primary institution of the new society. Perhaps it is not too much to say that if the business firm was the key institution of the past one hundred years because of its role in organizing production for the mass creation of products, the university will become the central institution of the next hun-

dred years because of its role as the new source of innovation and knowledge."

This book is an inquiry into the different sorts of relationships universities and professors have with the rest of
society, carried forward in large part to find out what
their impact is and whether there is anything to the no-
tion that the university is central to industrial activity.

The university industry basically consists of 2200 institutions, with total annual revenues of $10 billion and a
growth rate of some 10 percent. The business employs
half a million people as instructors, and holds 6.7 million
students. The shape of the industry changes, depending as
it does on the shifting alliances with government, which
supplies much of the money for research, and on business,
which makes the products resulting from the research.

It is difficult to gain any clear understanding of the university because it remains as one of the few large secret
organizations within the nation. One can find out more
about the activities of a public corporation than about a
university. The trustees of private universities are invariably self-perpetuating bodies of businessmen who meet in
private and do not publish accounts of their activities. In
public institutions, where there are more apt to be pe-
riodic open meetings of the regents and trustees who are
elected or appointed by the state governor, the real business goes on behind the scenes in executive sessions, and
the minutes of these back-room deals are either nonexis-
tent or never made public. Institutions of higher learning
are tax exempt, yet unlike the foundations which enjoy
the same status but are required by the Internal Revenue
Service to make public certain financial information, universities are not subject to such provisions. And so far as
the private colleges are concerned, the government allows
them to operate in total secrecy if they desire. Many of
the large private universities do publish financial reports
to reassure their alumni, but this is not a standard practice.
Columbia University will make available on request a list
of its securities investments but refuses to disclose real es-

tate holdings, a delicate matter since some of them are located in slum areas. The University of Chicago will not disclose any of its investments. Even though Long Island University, a private university, is chartered by the state of New York and numbers among its trustees a U.S. congressman, Ogden Reid, it refused to provide a financial report to a state legislative committee investigating its activities. The University of California, a public institution —the largest university in the world—with a budget of nearly $1 billion, steadfastly refused to disclose its holdings, and even the members of the regents committee which invests the money have expressed their ignorance of where it goes. At the University of Maryland the budget is figured with the administration by a planning bureau, which will not even make known the full details to different academic departments, on the general theory that if one department doesn't know what the others are getting, it won't be likely to argue about the course of university expansion.

While it is usual to distinguish between private and public universities, this can be misleading. Two thirds of American students go to public institutions, and the government spends large amounts of money in both types of schools, so much so that Clark Kerr, former president of the University of California, calls the modern university the "Federal Grant University."

In the Northwest Ordinance of 1787, the federal government set forth its intention of encouraging education, but as a practical matter this meant little until the passage of the Morrill Act of 1862 and subsequent legislation which provided land for public institutions and funds for instruction in agriculture. This led to the establishment of university-operated agricultural extension programs and farm experiment stations. In World War I the government spent a little money at universities for research in improving aircraft and established the ROTC programs for training officers. By the 1930's it was spending money for research in cancer through the creation of the National Cancer Institute. During the depression the universities assisted the government with New Deal public-works measures.

The U.S. government's involvement with the universities had a distinctly utilitarian bent, tied for the most part to industrial or military ends; by contrast, the European universities had become research centers. Consequently, many of the great scientists in the United States during the early part of the century were schooled abroad. Because of the demands of the second world war, the scientists and the military formed a working partnership which resulted first in dramatic scientific breakthroughs leading to the atomic bomb, and subsequently widened into the present pervasive relationship between government and all segments of the Academic Community.

The first controlled chain reaction which led to the development of the atomic bomb was achieved in laboratories at the University of Chicago. Johns Hopkins ran the Applied Physics Laboratory which developed the self-deteriorating proximity fuse. The Radiation Laboratory at MIT was the main center for radar research. During the period of the cold war the ties between university scientists and the government broadened and solidified. Many of the studies which led to the development of the hydrogen bomb were made by university scientists who spent their summers at Los Alamos; the father of the bomb, Edward Teller, of course, is from the University of California. The Lincoln Labs at MIT carried forward work on radar defense warning systems, as well as on missile guidance systems. The Jason Division of the Institute for Defense Analysis, a think tank run for the Defense Department by twelve universities, made studies for the military on missile re-entry problems, counter-insurgency and tactical uses of nuclear warfare in Southeast Asia. Professors at Harvard and MIT worked on building clever communications systems for the military, and others worked secretly during the summers on breaking codes. It was during the 1950's that the CIA began its covert financing through universities. It was interested in building up anti-communist student movements at home and creating anti-communist labor unions abroad.

Today more than two thirds of the university research funds come from the Department of Defense, the Atomic Energy Commission or the National Aeronautics and Space Administration, all closely concerned with defense matters. Much of this money is channeled to a small number of well-known universities. A congressional study in 1964 indicated that of 2100 universities, ten received 38 percent of the federal funds for research and development. (They are the University of California, MIT, Cornell, Columbia, University of Michigan, Harvard, Illinois, Stanford, Chicago and Minnesota.) This money often accounts for large portions of the universities' total budgets. Thus, 80 percent of MIT's funds are estimated to come from the government; Columbia and Princeton get about 50 percent of their money from Washington. In addition, there has been widespread covert funding by the CIA of university projects through front foundations.

The universities' growing liaison with the defense agencies over the past decade has coincided with the expanding importance of the Defense Department, which under Robert McNamara wandered rather far afield from military matters. The Defense Department, which bought the professors' expertise, helped shape the aerospace industry, then laid the groundwork for and supported the new education business. As a hedge against disarmament, the Defense Department encouraged the electronics firms which relied on it for business to get into other fields, one of which was to develop the computer for use in teaching children. The Defense planners also were leaders among those who pointed out that there might be businesses in slum rebuilding, water and air pollution abatement. The Defense Department helped write the poverty program, and when under the stewardship of Sargent Shriver it failed to meet expectations, McNamara sent along efficiency experts to restore order. McNamara's assistants were put in the Department of Health, Education and Welfare, where they remodeled it in imitation of the Pentagon. As they moved from one endeavor to the next, McNamara's staff towed along professors to add their expertise.

In a good many instances the liaisons between the defense agencies and the universities were accomplished through the federal contract research centers. There are forty-seven of them; the centers do $1.2 billion worth of research and development work annually, almost all of it sponsored by the Defense Department or the Atomic Energy Commission. Nearly half the money goes to centers managed by universities. The center idea has provided a convenient way for inveigling bright scientists into defense work. The government can pay the scientists higher wages by hiring them through universities, thereby getting around the civil service pay scales. As for the scientists themselves, they appear more distinguished to their colleagues as members of the faculty of some great university than if they were working on bomb sites in some dingy Pentagon office. And the centers give the universities a bit of prestige and a management fee. (Johns Hopkins gets $1 million annually in fees for administering the $50 million budget of the Applied Physics Laboratory.)

In theory, the government gets the best independent scientific advice in this manner, but in fact, what happens is that the major universities become first captive and then active advocates for the military and para-military agencies of government in order to get more money for research. This leads to bizarre situations; last spring Senator Fulbright, the chairman of the Senate Foreign Relations Committee, announced he had been denied certain information concerning the war in Vietnam, prepared for the Defense Department by the Institute for Defense Analysis, although the presidents of the sponsoring universities had access to it.

During the presidency of John Kennedy the Defense Department civilians were important in fashioning and implementing schemes for limited war and counter-insurgency, which resulted in the army's being viewed as an instrument of foreign policy in Southeast Asia and Latin America. Previously it had been widely assumed that the conduct of foreign affairs was the job of the State Department. Whereas during past wars the military relied on relatively straightforward methods of pitting armies against one another, during the Kennedy and early Johnson periods the civilians in the Defense Department got excited about the possibilities of using propaganda devices to manipulate the internal policies of foreign countries, and this in turn led to financing grandiose projects by university social scientists to study the behavior of the enemy, and involving foreign universities in the same work through grants. In 1968, the military will be spending approximately $50 million for projects related to developments in U.S. foreign policy. While there is some pressure within the Congress for stopping these projects, it is more likely that they will instead be expanded, for the social scientists have lately been smitten with what the Defense Department calls "Peacefare," ways of transposing the ideas and machinery employed by the military for civilian uses, such as counter-insurgency tactics in the ghetto, or teaching blacks to behave themselves by putting them all in the army, where, as Patrick Moynihan argues, they may learn a trade before being packed into a coffin in Vietnam.

It was through the Defense Department that the universities and business first worked together in consortia arrangements to develop complicated weapons systems. This troika arrangement is slowly evolving into a new sort of corporate machine, or more precisely, machine parts which engage or disengage depending on the job to be done. Basically, the parts consist of the university, where products or processes are conceived, the government, which finances their development, and private business, which makes and sells the finished item.

The emerging forms of corporate organization are very

much in flux, but the professor entrepreneurs, who dart back and forth from university to government to business, help shape corporate structures and policies.

The theory is that the activities of the corporations can be planned and set in motion by scholars who scheme together at their innards. Other scholars within the government make sure the goals of production are worthy, and to control the activity of the corporations, they ring changes through the economic machinery, as, for example, in the late Senator Robert Kennedy's slum rehabilitation plan. Its central feature is to bring outside economic support into the ghetto and yet promote the illusion of black control. In fact, the control remains with the large corporations, which in return for widening their power base are slightly more beneficent, hiring some blacks but passing on the cost of their involvement to the consumers through higher prices.

So the scholars dash back and forth, building the new economic and political machinery. They see themselves as renaissance men, the proprietors of the new factories.

2. The Directors

Since the end of World War II, American universities increasingly have come to look like new centers for industry. Whereas it was once common among radicals to view these institutions as captive technical schools, preparing workers to take up jobs in companies whose ideals were represented by the businessmen trustees, today it is apparent that the modern university more nearly resembles a conglomerate corporation on its own. There is a great sprawl of different enterprises: graduate institutes, computation centers, a propaganda headquarters for testing —where sociologists make up questionnaires and send them around the country to determine the citizenry's reaction to crucial political issues. In all likelihood there will be campuses in Madrid, Florence or Lima, and teams of researchers carrying out inquiries for AID or the CIA in Ethiopia or Thailand. The university will own a press, a ball park, a couple of hotels, some ships, and for complete diversification, an amusement park. Some go in for more exotic stuff: Purdue ran an airline for a time; Dartmouth has a timber-producing forest; Wesleyan put out the *Weekly Reader,* the sickening children's magazine, before selling it to Xerox for several million. The University of Wisconsin is responsible for the world's leading rat poison; NYU has a spaghetti factory; and there are persistent reports, denied, that Yale is in the bra business.

The modern institution of higher education is likely to be interlocked with a defense-system laboratory or AEC in-

9

stallation, located near the campus and surrounded by a sprawl of companies begun by professors who developed with public funds in the university's laboratories the products they now sell for private gain.

Like any other big government contractor, the university does not require salesmen to negotiate the contracts, relying instead on contacts with a former professor who is on leave of absence to run a research section of the Defense Department. And like any large industrial corporation, the university retains a Washington lobbyist to influence legislation in the Congress. The University of California has an office full of people in Washington who follow legislation.

At first the new organizational arrangements developed around the defense electronics business, but now it is not uncommon to find the "spin-offs," as the professors' companies are called, selling educational games and proposing to run Job Corps camps or schools for small children. They are deeply involved in "social problems," running community development centers in the slums, preparing a "menu" of options to better motivate laggard black businessmen or inviting people in to play a game which will help show them where a new superhighway should go.

Deans and presidents take a benign view of this sort of activity, often encouraging the professor to start a new company, and once begun, sitting on its board of directors or that of a local bank, where they can lend a hand in financing and coordinating the whole works. Since a spin-off is generally begun at least because of an invention or theory coming out of a university laboratory, the new company seeks to keep in touch with its source, sometimes by making sure the professor involved continues to teach or acts as a consultant.

One result of all this is to change the function of the university's central administration. Whereas at the beginning of the century universities were still run by towering men with messianic views, they are now operated by teams of middle management executives, who often see themselves as labor mediators. They run what in effect is a kind of data-processing center: part bank, to provide the money for the activities of the different subsidiaries; part brokerage, for arranging deals among quarreling faculty members or between a faculty group and the government. The undergraduates, for their part, lie in holding pens, off the labor market, providing the rationale for financing the university. The old graduate students, of course, provide cheap labor pools, useful for keeping the undergraduates in hand and for assisting the senior professors in carrying forward their inquiries both within the university or in some private company. Teaching classes of undergraduate students is not especially interesting compared to working on the outside in one of the new companies, and the professors tell you it is obsolete as well: the students learn more by working in the "real world laboratory," which is to say on some professor's experiment outside the university. Professors once sneered at businessmen and the profit motive, but since they have been so successful in taking up the game themselves, the profit motive is now approvingly referred to as the "reward structure." Business activities are now a subject fit for study, and have given rise to the myth of the "entrepreneur." (How do you make people entrepreneurs? How and why do small entrepreneurs group together "to grow" a new industry?)

As Leonard Duhl, a special assistant to the Secretary of Health, Education and Welfare, observes, out of all this emerges a sort of triangular power system. The money flows out of the government down to the university, where someone hatches a utilitarian idea, and from there over to a company which either makes a product or designs a test. The object of the university game, then, is to control any two legs of the triangle, for by doing so, the university professor can establish the beginnings of power.

The models for the new industrial arrangement are to be

found at Stanford University in Palo Alto, California, in the small towns near Cambridge, Massachusetts, and along Route 128, where the professors leaving MIT and Harvard established a successful defense elctronics business. While the MIT and Harvard people simply left the universities to start companies around Cambridge, there is a more complex and grandiose arrangement at Stanford. The university was left 9000 acres of land by Leland Stanford, the railroad tycoon who founded the place; a good part of this land is now an industrial park which houses fifty companies, all involved in research and development. They keep in close touch with the university's electronics laboratory, which pioneered developments in the vacuum tube and microwave equipment. The relationships are not especially subtle. Glynn Mapes, in the *Wall Street Journal,* describes the origins of Barry Research Corporation, one of the companies that sprang from the electronics laboratories. George Barry is a radio engineer and physicist who worked in the laboratory. Two of his colleagues figured out a way to measure an area covered by a radio broadcast for the Voice of America. When the agency asked Stanford to find a manufacturer to produce the device, Barry quit his job as professor, and with his colleagues helping out in their spare time, started the company and submitted the winning bid. Another Stanford scientist helped the government to evaluate the proposal. He told Mapes, "Naturally we weren't averse to [Mr. Barry's] winning the award. He was and still is one of the top experts in the field."

Stanford realizes $1 million a year in leases from the companies, and it operates, as a subsidiary, the Stanford Research Institute, a non-profit research organization which grosses $25 million a year and has offices around the world. Attracted by all this activity, another two hundred companies hunker about the edges of Palo Alto.

Universities seeking to copy the Stanford model have met with mixed results. Cornell, which is stuck out in the woods of upper New York State, tried the same thing, but the one main client, General Electric, pulled out and the venture all but collapsed. On the other hand, the Research Triangle at Raleigh-Durham, a conglomerate of Duke University, North Carolina State and the University of North Carolina, flourishes. The University of Illinois has a going research institute. The University of Minnesota joined with industrialists in the upper Middle West to form the North Star Research Institute, which was supposed to produce the ideas to galvanize the economy of that region, but so far as anyone can tell, it has turned out to be little more than a repository for classified research projects the university would rather not get directly involved in. Purdue set up an industrial park, but from all accounts it is a dismal failure. If they are successful, the research institutes often turn into big clumsy affairs, preparing never-ending streams of boring studies which are thrown away; nonetheless, they provide useful fronts for professors who want to carry out secret or proprietary research that their university otherwise prevents them from doing.

Most of the spin-offs around Cambridge came into being because professors left MIT laboratories to start them. Studies undertaken by Edward Roberts and Herbert A. Wainer of Lincoln Labs, which works on radar defense systems, and the Instrumentation Laboratory, which developed the guidance system for the Apollo missile, indicate that eighty different companies were begun by people who left. These two labs account for half of MIT's budget. Another twenty-seven companies were started by professors departing other MIT labs, and fifty-nine firms were traced to men coming out of the academic departments. While the bulk of sales for these firms at first comes from government contracts, Roberts maintains that after four or five years, 40 percent of the business is in commercial markets. Roberts found that the new companies needed very little capital to begin with, usually starting on personal savings of a few thousand dollars. Once operating, they were able to tap ample sources of risk capital around Boston, through organizations like American Research & Development Corporation, Laurance Rockefeller, Polaroid Corporation or the Boston banks that gamble on new business.

While the industrial park-cum-research institute is a hit-or-miss proposition, there are vastly successful spin-offs all around the country. To give a few examples: Tracor, Incorporated, was begun by University of Texas professors and makes $50 million a year, much of it by working on defense systems. Dr. Norman Hackerman, president of the Austin campus of the university and former head of the chemistry department, said he used to shuttle business to Tracor, and worked there as a consultant. Princeton is the center of a flourishing research and development business. While the university itself is cool to the idea of professors doing too much on the side, there are several firms begun by professors who still remain on university staffs as "visiting lecturers." Richard M. Colgate, of the soap family, financed Applied Logic Corporation, which he began with James R. Guard, a professor on leave from Princeton, and Thomas H. Mott, Jr., of the Rutgers faculty. Applied Logic makes programs for time-shared computers; five other Princeton professors work in one way or the other for the firm. While Dartmouth College in Hanover, New Hampshire, is off the main line, Thermal Dynamics, a firm that makes special cutting torches, was formed by a professor. Another company, Time Share Corporation, opened offices near Hanover because of the work in computer development going on at the college. Moreover, Dartmouth exchanges personnel with Crel, the army's cold-weather research laboratory, which is nearby.

Sixteen spin-off companies have been established since 1950 around the Ann Arbor campus of the University of Michigan, and the state legislature gives the university money so it can drum up more money for these businesses. Probably the best known of them is Conductron, established in 1960 by Keeve M. Siegel, then a professor of electrical engineering at the university. Initially, Siegel received permission from Harlan Hatcher, the president of the University of Michigan, and even after the company was going, Siegel remained for several years on the university's faculty. Conductron makes radar and optical equipment, and its motto is "In Talent We Trust." The development of this company shows clearly how the new spin-offs and established universities work to one another's advantage. To begin the enterprise, Siegel took twenty-five people away from the university—fifteen of them professors, most of whom continued as faculty members even while working for the company. Then Conductron shuttled $250,000 of research into the engineering department, where several members of the company's staff still maintained their jobs as professors. At the same time the university handed out a $39,000 subcontract to Conductron. The University of Michigan laboratories performed advanced research in detection of underground explosions; Conductron applied these techniques in making machinery for detecting and evaluating data from underground explosions in drilling for oil. In 1966 Siegel sold control of the company to McDonnell-Douglas, the aircraft company, and started another firm. He is estimated to have made $5 million on Conductron.

Conductron begins to show the sort of political leverage a professor can obtain by working in two organizations at once. In an earlier time it was crucial to control patents to inventions, but as work on this patent is eroded, the man with a competitive edge needs to be inside the organization where the idea originates, and he needs to form a sort of consortium between the university, or department of a university, and a company in order to exploit it.

There are other ways in which universities as organizations and professors within them have worked toward this sort of relationship. While Dartmouth is opposed in policy to performing secret military research on the campus, its engineering school permits students to work on proprietary research for companies so they can learn development techniques. Southern Methodist University hires industrialists as adjunct professors from companies like General Dynamics and Texas Instruments. Classes are televised, and are watched by students on the campus as well as by company employees who take the course as part of their work. Princeton is changing the rules of its engineering department to permit up to one quarter of its graduate students to be in attendance only part time, and certain courses are televised for the benefit of employees at the nearby RCA laboratory. Stanford encourages neighboring companies to send their people to school; the students pay the regular tuition and the companies make matching payments to the university. Northeastern University in Boston has developed special part-time programs for people working in the Route 128 complex.

While Princeton has rules against classified research and excessive consulting, and publicly states it is against secret research of any sort, it nevertheless finds ways to dodge around this. One of them is through Textile Research Institute, which dates back to 1944. The institute is financed by the textile companies and Princeton professors carry on proprietary work there. TRI awards scholarships plus tuition to students at the Princeton graduate school, and appears to handle the admissions blanks to both the institute and the university, and TRI then recommends those students it regards as eligible for admission. Fellowships are renewed "contingent only upon satisfactory performance in his academic studies at Princeton University and in his research work at TRI." As for the graduate student's research, "the research topic is chosen jointly by the student, the faculty members under whose guidance the research is to be conducted *and the institute*." (Italics added.) Many of the subjects for research are suggested by the institute; and when any of the company-financed research results in patentable inventions, these become its property.

In other, perhaps more old-fashioned ways, universities

have obtained for themselves some political influence by going into business other than education. It is common for universities in small towns to control local business institutions, especially the banks. Princeton controls or owns outright the two main hotels, the movie theater and stores on the main street of Princeton; in addition, it has bought up thousands of acres of land stretching behind the university to keep it from being inundated by strip developments. Its representatives are on both local banks. The treasurer of Dartmouth College is chairman of the Hanover Trust Company, where Dartmouth has an account, and the college owns the inn and several buildings on the main street in town. Both Harvard and MIT have their representatives in many of the banks in Cambridge, Massachusetts. The University of Michigan helped finance the building of a Howard Johnson's near the campus in Ann Arbor.

In the past, universities have been heavily involved in the real estate business. Columbia owns the land under Rockefeller Center. The University of Chicago holds valuable sites in the downtown Loop area of that city. The University of California dabbles in oil and gas leases around the country.

Northwestern University at Evanston, Illinois, operates under a peculiar charter which permits it to pass on a tax break to large corporations in the Chicago area. Northwestern's charter was drawn before Illinois became a state, and then endorsed by the state legislature in 1851. It exempts the university from paying taxes on any land it owns. This is usual where educational institutions use land for "educational purposes," but Northwestern is exempted from taxes on all land. It therefore has entered into liaisons with large corporations, buying commercial sites from them, then leasing them back, thereby providing them with a loophole to avoid paying property taxes. The commercial enterprise first needs to place real estate in trust, then the trustee improves the land. Next he enters into lease arrangements with the company, which all along holds real control of the property. Then Northwestern purchases the property from the trustee, and along with it, the long-term lease arrangement. From then on the property is tax-exempt. The university holds $41.8 million, or 17 percent of its investment portfolio, in real estate, and has lease-back deals with Wilson & Company, the meat packers, Illinois Bell Telephone Company, Phillips Petroleum, National Biscuit Company and Kroger Company. Cook County States Attorney's Office is suing to make the university pay $155,000 in back taxes for 1963 alone. In its suit, the county asks why Northwestern should be so diligent in protecting the rights of commercial organizations. The county is especially interested in the university's lease-back to Pepsi-Cola General Bottlers for a bottling plant outside Evanston. On September 30, 1967, Northwestern held $878,575 of Pepsico, Incorporated, common stock, and $298,572 of Pepsi-Cola General Bottlers. Students have often been curious as to why they seemingly couldn't buy anything but Pepsi soft drinks on the campus and at football games. But the university denies there is a deal and says Pepsi had the franchise for the stadium in the early 1960's. "The decision to change to Pepsi was based solely on matters of dollars and cents," William S. Kerr, the university's business manager, told the *Daily Northwestern*.

One of the most useful ways to chart the intermingling of interests of business and the university is to examine the large number of university officials who sit on boards of directors of large business corporations. As John Kenneth Galbraith suggests, this is a measure of the corporation's interest in the uses of the university, for by now the corporation accepts notions of planning and new ideas, and, indeed, the appearance of some military man or a university official on the board of directors is assurance to the stockholders that the corporation is up on the latest trends in government spending and technological development. From the university's point of view, the president who straddles both enterprises can begin to exercise some power on his own.

Franklin D. Murphy, who until 1968 was the chancellor of the University of California's Los Angeles campus, was equally well known as an educator and businessman. He sat on the boards of Ford Motor Company, Hallmark Cards, Inc., McCall Corporation and the Times-Mirror Company, which publishes the *Los Angeles Times*. In the latter two instances, the companies were represented on the university's board of regents. During a long talk Murphy described what he believed to be the growing relationship between universities and industrial organizations.

"The facts are that the best university professors from the best universities in the United States are usually involved in industry: as consultants, in the economic field, in the scientific field, in the management field, in the data-processing-systems analysis field—and this is growing rather than decreasing. It is a reflection on the part of modern industrial management that they can't fly by the seat of their pants and they do need this expertise, and a big infusion of it. And this creates some serious problems with the university because there is a limit to what any human being can do. If you have got your professors running around consulting all over the place, they are not around to talk to students. If you can keep it under control, and I think that there are ways that you can manage this at the university level, this is enormously valuable from my point of view. Number one, it does provide this necessary expertise (something that the French and the Germans want to talk to us about—how to strengthen university relationships with industry when both need it). Secondly, it does provide for the university professor the technique of guaranteeing to some degree that he will not be in an ivory tower and that he will be dealing in the teaching process with things that are germane and contemporary, not entirely theoretical. The students today are talking about relevancy, they want more relevance in it. And the way to get relevance in it is to have people who by personal experience know what's going on in the real world.

"I think that the reason that I am on the board of the Ford Motor Company is because in the conversations that go forward in the board of a complicated, world-wide enterprise like this, manpower requirements, not only in the United States, but in Germany and England and in Latin America—the Ford Motor Company has major installations in every part of the world—manpower requirements frequently come up. And frankly, I am able to make a contribution—I know people who are running universities or research institutions in different parts of the world, out of my own set of responsibilities, and I can be of practical value.

"Secondly, as a citizen living in the nonbusiness academic world, I can bring to the board some of the nontechnical but terribly important pressures or concerns of the society generally. For example, I am sure I am the most articulate person on the board about the public responsibility of the corporation, which in these days, in the case of Con Ed or Ford, has to do with pollution of the air. The fact is that we can't wait for government, that this is a public responsibility. Or the question of safety as it pertains to the automobile industry. You serve as a public representative in an interesting sort of way—if you are a good one, you are forthright, and you are candid and you can say, 'Look, fellows, from a financial point of view that is probably sound, from an engineering point of view it is probably sound, but have you put in the factor of the public?' So here I think I am useful.

"Thirdly, I think that over and beyond these technical contributions I am among other things a medical fellow. (Murphy is a physician.) I have instinctive reactions to our biological systems working with engineering systems, and here again I can and have made some positive suggestions and contributions as a board member. Then I have, of course, the common responsibility of any board member; namely, to see to it that there is prudency in management and mismanagement.

"What I get from it is contact with the real world. I am managing a hundred-million-dollar operation here at UCLA. I've learned an enormous amount and gotten an enormous number of insights, as I see a highly sophisticated corporate management with a ten-billion-dollar set of realities. So that especially in the managerial area I remain alert to and become associated with important managerial techniques and realities. So that I have become a better chancellor in terms of my managerial responsibilities.

"How much time do I give to it [Ford]? Well, I attend roughly ten meetings a year in Detroit—nine in Dearborn and we usually have one in one of our major installations around the country. That means I give up two days, ten times a year, so twenty days. In the interim, I am sent materials of one kind or another, which I faithfully read, examine and study. This is in my weekends, that is to say, reading time. I find it enormously stimulating. I come back to my old job fresh, with different ideas, and I think I act from time to time as a very useful goad and a very useful stimulant to our people in the corporate realm."

I asked Murphy what he was paid for doing this, and he replied, "It is two hundred fifty dollars a meeting plus a retainer of ten thousand dollars. But frankly, I do not do it for the money. Because to fly on an airplane twice in two days, ten days a year—there just isn't that much money when you have an income tax to pay. If it weren't very stimulating and useful to me, I wouldn't be doing it at all.

"Now McCall's is different. Here I have in a certain way been able to be even more useful. McCall's manages three magazines—the *Saturday Review* is the one that I am most interested in and that stimulates me a little. Here I am able to make a lot of suggestions about format, content, kinds of stories that should be covered, editorial thrust, things of this sort. For example, there was a story in there once a while back called 'The Day the Mails Stopped,' about the big Chicago mix-up. Well, this was specifically my suggestion—even the title. I pushed the thought that there should be an issue on California, because they could do it in a somewhat different way. On telling them what there should be in the issue—you don't tell Norman Cousins anything, you just suggest.

"I'm on four boards, and all of them I find fascinating. They're different and stimulating in their different ways. I've mentioned two. The third one that I would mention is the Times-Mirror Company here in Los Angeles. It has as its most important property, as you know, the *Los Angeles Times,* which in my prejudiced view, and I try to be objective, is one of the two or three greatest newspapers in the country. And it has been a wonderful thing to be a part of it. At present, and during its transformation period, I think I have been somewhat helpful there. This is in Los Angeles, there are only four meetings that don't quite take up the time, although there are interim meetings that I have where I can talk to others. And I am on the board of Hallmark Cards, which as you know is the largest greeting-card firm in the world. This goes back in history. This is a Kansas City-based company, and I grew up in Kansas City. Joyce Hall, who fathered it, asked me to go on the board—I was the first outside director ever to go on the board. And I am the oldest outside director on that board. This is a company in which I would say that I can make very little by way of contribution in a technical sense, but I have made quite a lot in a corporate management sense because in a privately held company there are different kinds of problems in management and structure of management. I am a close personal family friend and I think I have been rather helpful with certain critical points, in this regard. At least they think so. I go to Kansas City four times a year for this. And I see Mr. Hall quite often. He has a place here in California where he spends half the year, and I go there and we talk about things.

"I don't get paid on the Hallmark board at all. The Times-Mirror board is a hundred dollars a meeting and there is a small retainer—far from a lucrative point of view. The McCall board is less than the Ford board, it's somewhere between Times-Mirror and Ford."

Murphy calls himself a moderate Republican and took the view in the early days of Ronald Reagan's regime that the governor might be "civilized," which is another way of hoping he could be hauled around to become a middle-of-the-road liberal. Murphy himself was a considerable power in the university, having successfully argued for its decentralization, which, of course, worked to his benefit, giving him autonomy at UCLA, the largest campus in the university system. He was widely regarded as a major contender to become president when Clark Kerr was sacked by the regents. But in the end Murphy lost out to Charles J. Hitch, McNamara's former assistant and systems analyst, whom the regents regarded as the most placid person available at the time and least likely to disturb the governor who was trying to hack up the university's budget. In 1968, after Murphy had lost out to Hitch, and with Reagan still fighting the university, Murphy quit UCLA to become president of the Times-Mirror Company.

About one quarter of the 200 largest concerns listed in *Fortune*'s top 500 industrial corporations have university officials on their boards of directors. Six of the ten largest life insurance and utility companies have university representatives on their boards; so do five of the largest merchandising companies and four of the biggest transportation companies. University officials, on the other hand, are scarce on the boards of large banks.

(Life insurance companies seem especially interested in university people, often having two or three representatives on the board. One survey indicates that of the 350 insurance professors in the country, over half either consult or teach part time for the industry. Which may well help to explain why there is so little interest in correcting abuses in the insurance industry.)

Most of the university directors hold stock in the various companies, and are paid fees ranging anywhere from $2000 to $10,000 plus expenses for coming to meetings —which are often held monthly. Usually college people say they become company directors to see what life is like on the outside, and to make wealthy friends whom they can touch in fund-raising drives later on. (This is largely nonsense, for the bulk of money for private and public higher education comes from student tuition, state and federal government, not from industry.) The university president, in return, can usually help businessmen in recruiting efforts. In addition, educators are useful to corporations which must maintain large industrial training programs for their staffs. What is especially interesting in all this is that the businessmen come to judge a university president's abilities by his shrewd advice to the company, not because of how he runs the university.

I wrote to several board chairmen and asked them for their opinions as to what sort of contribution university officials were making to their firms, whether they thought from their point of view it was worthwhile, and what if anything the university was getting out of the deal. Most of the replies weren't especially helpful. "Their [educators'] approach to problems is often humanistic or historical and helps keep directives and decisions in perspective. Their concern with advancing the dignity of man is also a very useful input into corporate decisions," according to Thomas J. Watson, Jr., of IBM. "Although it is difficult to generalize about the role of prominent educators in advancing the interests of industry," says Henry Ford II, "I believe there is growing recognition of the need for deeper involvement of the university in day-to-day social and economic affairs. Whether it be through directorships in industry, through well-planned education-industry discussion programs or through a variety of other means, this commitment by the university to a larger role in the community would very definitely serve the interests of society."

Fortunately, it is possible to be more specific than this. Grayson Kirk, then at Columbia, helped IBM with education, which is estimated to cost $60 million a year, half as large as Columbia's annual budget. The Watson family always has had affection for Columbia, and the company gave the university $1.5 million for its most recent fund-raising drive. Kirk also sits on the board of Consolidated Edison Company; about the time Con Ed came through with a large gift, Charles F. Luce, its chairman, was made a Columbia trustee. In addition, Kirk sits on the board of the Greenwich Savings Bank, two small-ish mutual funds—Dividend Shares and Nationwide Securities—and is a director of Socony Mobil, where he takes charge of an employee-incentive scheme. The chairman of Socony Mobil is Albert L. Nickerson, who is a member of the Harvard Corporation, a self-perpetuating group of six men that governs the university. Kirk has about $50,000 of stocks in these various companies, and he gets fees for attending the board meetings. James Killian, chairman of the board at MIT, sits on the General Motors board. Killian says he resisted the entreaties of his friend Alfred Sloan, who wanted him to go on the company's board some years ago. At the time Killian was president of MIT and felt it improper for the chief executive officer to be on a company board. However, on becoming chairman of the institute, he gave in to the arm-twisting and went along. Howard Johnson, now the president of MIT, sits on the boards of Federated Department Stores and John Hancock Insurance Company, among others. Jerome Weisner, former head of the President's Science Advisory Committee under President Kennedy, is the provost at MIT, and he has been picked up as a director by several companies, including Celanese Corporation. The apparent all-time winner in this business is Jess

Davis, president of Stevens Institute of Technology, who sits on the boards of seven large companies: Carrier Corporation, Philip Morris, National Biscuit Company, Bethlehem Steel, Prudential Insurance, First National Bank of Jersey City and Public Service Electric and Gas Company.

Nathan M. Pusey, the president of Harvard, does not sit on company boards. Neither does Kingman Brewster, Jr., president of Yale, who says, "It's a frightful waste of time."

Brewster, the consummate politician, always mindful of preserving the image of respectable New England Republicanism, believes it is wrong for a university official to be on the board of directors of a local bank or public utility. He thinks that as a matter of sound business practice, one should be in a position to drive as hard a bargain as possible, and sitting as both university official and bank director is compromising. How could one argue for a good deal for the university, when as a director of the bank you would be trying to chisel your stockholders out of profits?

Shortly after Brewster told me this, John Ecklund, treasurer of Yale, said that Charles O'Hearn, Brewster's assistant, sat on the board of the First New Haven Bank, where Yale maintains its principal account.

Robert F. Goheen, president of Princeton, is on the board of Equitable Life Assurance Society, which has an $11 million policy with the university. James Oates, the Equitable chairman, is also a Princeton trustee and heads the trustee executive committee. Goheen was vague about his work for Equitable, but Oates said Goheen helped the company in several ways. For one thing, when Equitable got interested in financing construction at a university, they could call on the president of Princeton University to provide an estimate as to the excellence of the school, what its future was in terms of education. In addition, Oates said Goheen made valuable suggestions for the board of directors, almost all of the men he proposed having been made directors. And Oates found his relations with Goheen useful for another reason. Students are not very friendly to business these days, and Goheen can help arrange conferences for Oates on the Princeton campus, giving him the chance to talk quietly to the students and persuade them that business is not so dreadful.

These relationships give Goheen real leverage. Because of his affiliation with Equitable, he is more important in the university world, since he always must be considered as a potential source for raising funds; on the other hand, he wields influence within the business community, because he knows about universities, which the businessmen see as good long-term investments. This sort of prestige and power can widen if, in fact, other members of the board owe their jobs as directors of Equitable Life Assurance Society to the president of Princeton University.

T. Keith Glennan, former president of Case Western Reserve University, now the president of Associated Universities, Incorporated, the consortia which manages Brookhaven National Laboratories, is on the board of directors of Republic Steel Corporation. The chairman of the company, T. F. Patton, explains how Glennan and Republic worked together: "His membership on Republic's board strengthened the ties between Republic and Case Western Reserve University [formerly Case Institute of Technology]. As a result, Republic is in constant communication with the faculty of Case with respect to research in metallurgy, recruiting of able students and holding seminars on matters in areas of importance to the corporation. Because of his membership on our board, Republic has taken a particular interest in the field of metallurgy, and by its financial assistance has enabled Case to establish one of the finest metallurgy departments available in any university in the country. Republic has established a chair of metallurgy at Case, which is filled with some of the greatest metallurgical minds from all parts of the world.

"On an informal basis," Patton continued, "I discussed

with Dr. Glennan what the role of the company should be in the years ahead—should it confine its activities to steel alone, should it be looking into other materials, what kinds of steel will be needed to meet the requirements of the space age, should the company branch out into other fields than that of materials? Dr. Glennan is also very helpful in making suggestions concerning relationships between the company and government, and the steel industry and government, and in advising what steps should be taken to improve these important relationships."

W. Clarke Wescoe, president of the University of Kansas, sits on the Phillips Petroleum board, and he has helped the company set up more efficient recruitment policies. As a Phillips director, Wescoe got to know more people, and as a consequence he was put on other boards of directors. N. S. Adams, chairman of the Phillips board, says, "I am satisfied that the friendships established, and the additional income which he therefore has received, may have materially influenced his decision to stay at the University of Kansas when he was wooed by the University of Minnesota this past year. The vice-chairman of our board, Mr. Stanley Learned, is chairman of a special committee for fund raising at the University of Kansas at this time. I doubt that he would have taken this assignment had not Dr. Wescoe been a member of our board."

Dealings between business institutions and university officials, as in the case of Eugene Power, a regent of the University of Michigan from 1956 to 1965, caused a row in that state.

Power had founded and was president of University Microfilms, which sells microfilm copies of out-of-date and rare books and now is a subsidiary of Xerox. Power is a staunch Democrat, and in 1965 was a university regent as well as president of the American Association of University Governing Boards. In October, 1965 Roger Rapoport revealed in the campus newspaper, *The Michigan Daily*, that University Microfilms and the University of Michigan enjoyed a close relationship. The facts were confirmed by Frank Kelley, State Attorney General. When a graduate student completed his thesis, he took it to the library, where according to regulations a microfilm negative of the work was made and stored away with the others in a special place. If anyone ever wanted a copy, the university would make one up, charging certain established rates. The university librarians spent $50,000 in culling 400,000 books to select 40,000 for an undergraduate library. When completed, this shelf-list became highly regarded and was widely imitated in other libraries.

University Microfilms then moved in and copied the shelf-list, and using the name of the university in advertisements ("How the Students at Arizona State Used the University of Michigan Library Shelf-List"), sold it publicly for its own gain. In card-catalogue form the list sold for $1900 and in book form for $875. The microfilm company did not ask the university's permission to use its name in advertising, nor did it pay the school any royalties. In addition, the library was, in fact, giving the microfilm negatives of the thesis to Power's company, which stored them and sold the reproductions for its own profit. Finally, the company put its cameras in the basement of the library, where it could photograph fragile or rare books which could not be taken out of the building.

Subsequent to these revelations, Frank Kelley made an investigation and determined that there was "substantial conflict of interest" by Power in his business dealings with the university. (The university regents, incidentally, made their own study, which showed there was no conflict of interest.) At this point Power left the board. Kelley said, "There is no question of Mr. Power's motives, his integrity or his devotion to the interest of the university . . ." He added, however, "for Mr. Power to maintain his position as a Regent while his company has its present relationship with the university is inconsistent with the requirements of the Michigan Constitution relating to 'substantial conflict of interest.' " Harlan Hatcher, the president of the institution, said, "It is indeed a harsh choice that deprives the state of Mr. Power's direct services to the university and to higher education."

Conflict of interest by university officials and board members was very much of a political issue by February of 1967, when Rapoport was proposed by the senior staff of the *Michigan Daily* as the next editor. Recommendation of an editor goes to the board in control of student publications, which consists of students, faculty, administrators and alumni. In practice, the board has for twenty-five years routinely accepted the nominations. But this time they found Rapoport to be "unacceptable." The vote was seven to four, with students and one faculty member for Rapoport; the administrators and others against him. The *Michigan Daily* then reported that Hatcher told the chairman of the board that he was displeased by the choice of Roger Rapoport. After this story appeared, Hatcher said one of his responsibilities as president "is to convey to the board in control of student publications the concern of the Regents. This I have done." Hatcher said he tried not to interfere with student newspapers, "pained as I have been at times by its youthful harshness, and by the occasional damage to the university which I and others have labored quietly to repair."

The university administration had talked three previous editors of the *Daily* out of running the story on Power on the grounds that he was doing more good than harm.

By September, 1967, Kelley interpreted the new conflict-of-interest law, passed by the legislature at his request, to mean that officers and directors of banks and companies that do business with state colleges cannot sit on the school boards. (However, he ruled that a university officer or board member who sat as director of a state-regulated public utility furnishing service to a college or university was not in a conflict of interest.) This forced resignations of several people. Hatcher quit his job as director of the Ann Arbor bank where the university keeps its payroll. John A. Hannah, president of Michigan

State, resigned as director of two banks: Manufacturers National Bank of Detroit and the American Bank & Trust Company of Lansing. Six trustees at Eastern Michigan University and Western Michigan who sat on boards of banks that did business with those universities quit as trustees of the schools. And six other university officials, including the presidents of Central Michigan and Eastern Michigan, resigned as bank directors.

No sooner had this shake-up taken place than the *Michigan Daily* unearthed another interesting involvement between university officers and outside business interests. This one involved Hannah and Philip Jesse May, the treasurer at Michigan State.

This was a series of tricky deals: May got a $165,000 loan in 1955 from the Lincoln National Life Insurance Company, through the Ann Arbor Trust Company, for construction of a building in Lansing by Philip Jesse Company, whose officers included May's wife and brothers. Lincoln National writes insurance for the MSU faculty; Ann Arbor Trust has MSU accounts. The sole occupant of the building until June, 1967, was IBM. MSU did some $500,000 of business a year with IBM. That month IBM moved into a new building near the campus. A $1.1 million mortgage loan was secured through the Michigan National Bank, where MSU had its main account and where until Kelley's ruling May had been a director. After IBM moved out of the first building, May tried to rent it to the State Department of Education, but Kelley kept him from doing so by ruling that a state officer can't contract with the state. May somehow leased instead to the probate court. MSU trustees heard about May's deals, and there was pressure for his resignation. But Hannah, president of the school, stood strongly behind the treasurer, declaring that if May went, so would he.

May also was on the board of the Walter Neller Realty Company in Lansing, which had purchased 180 acres of land near the MSU campus in the summer of 1967 from Hannah. Hannah said he originally bought the land for retirement but was forced to sell because of high taxes. May insisted he had never discussed Hannah's property with Neller Realty.

Then the *Michigan State News*, the MSU newspaper, printed a story disclosing that from 1950 to 1958 more than $900,000 in MSU construction contracts went to the Vandenburg Construction Company. The president of this firm was Hannah's brother-in-law, who subsequently went out of business and turned up as the construction superintendent at MSU. Hannah was quoted as saying at the trustee's meeting, "It's true that Vandenburg is my brother-in-law, but I didn't know he was employed by the university." He also said, "As far as I know he never did a job for this institution. I was surprised by the figure . . . I smell what's coming on. This is an attempt at discrediting the university by discrediting me."

Subsequent to these disclosures, May took a six-month leave of absence at full pay to study business practices in higher education.

3. The University Business

One of the more interesting features of the university is its conception of itself as a new-style investment trust. In his 1966 annual report, McGeorge Bundy, President of the Ford Foundation, said that the foundation had set up a committee to examine the management and investment practices of universities with an eye to helping them get better performance from their endowment funds. These now total $12 billion. One novel possibility was that Ford might help some of the smaller colleges in pooling their endowments into a kind of mutual fund. Then, they might stalk the securities markets with several billion dollars instead of a few million and that way gain some leverage. This is another way for universities to gain some measure of power in the society. Harvard and Yale provide examples of how this sort of thing can work out.

Decisions as to where and how to invest Harvard's $1 billion endowment fund are made on advice of the treasurer by the six members of the self-perpetuating corporation which runs the university. The treasurer is George F. Bennett, who also is president of State Street Investment Corporation. State Street manages three mutual funds with assets of $600 million, and it also handles investments for Harvard. Francis H. Burr, a partner in the law firm of Ropes & Gray, also sits on the boards of both the Harvard Corporation and the State Street Investment Corporation. Bennett, thus, in addition to being paid as president of the investment company, also draws a small

33

SMALL

fee, said to be $25,000 a year, from Harvard for invest-
ment advice. When Bennett's company sees a good investment, it will often buy for both the mutual funds and
Harvard. While Bennett's mutual funds in themselves are
not especially large as the size of these funds goes, when
he combines them with the $600,000,000 that is available
in Harvard's endowment fund for stock investment, he
enters the market with a leverage of $1.2 billion. The ar-
rangement between State Street and Harvard was initially
set up by State Street's founder, Paul C. Cabot, who
preceded Bennett as treasurer of the university. When
Cabot entered into this arrangement, it was specified that
when it came to buying and selling securities held by both
Harvard and the State Street mutual funds, the funds
would lead in buying or selling; so at least in theory, Bennett can purchase a stock for State Street Investment and
drive it up by using Harvard's money to buy. Or, in selling, he can dump a large holding belonging to State Street
and then sell Harvard on a lower market. However, Bennett claims it never works out like this, and that, oddly,
Harvard often does much better than State Street.

Harvard is involved in one potentially embarrassing situation as a result of this investment combine. Both Harvard and State Street hold large blocks of stock in Middle
South Utilities, Incorporated, a holding company which
controls electric utilities in various southern states, including companies in Mississippi and Louisiana. State
Street owns 485,000 of Middle South common stock; Harvard has 543,719 shares; Harvard-Yenching Institute, an
organization devoted to promoting higher education in
Asia, of which Bennett is deputy treasurer, has 18,668
shares; Bennett himself holds 2,000 shares and is a director of the company. This is obviously in part by virtue of
the large holdings he represents, and in part because he
helped set up the company. In recent years Harvard undergraduates unsuccessfully challenged the university's
Middle South stock holdings on the grounds that the
southern companies were managed by racists, members of

the Klan and White Citizens Councils, and that through its financial support Harvard was in fact aiding segregation. Bennett says he regards these utilities as public service companies, regulated under state laws: "I made a personal investigation, and satisfied myself that the officers were law-abiding citizens." When he was asked about the investment at a public meeting, Dr. Pusey declared, "If there are discriminatory practices, then the company should be prosecuted under federal law." When the students hissed at this, Pusey added, "Our purpose is just to invest in places that are selfishly good for Harvard. We do not use our money for social purposes."

Yale wants to get the same leverage as Harvard by building a similar trust. In the fall of 1967 Yale announced the establishment of an investment advisory firm called Endowment Management & Research Corporation, which will manage the university's $500 million in endowment funds. The president, Roland D. Grimm, and all the other operating officers are either Yale or Harvard graduates with experience in managing mutual funds. They sit as directors of the company along with three Yale trustees: J. Richardson Dilworth, chairman of the university's finance committee and a prestigious investment banker of Philadelphia, who now works with Rockefeller Family & Associates; William W. Scranton, former governor of Pennsylvania; and John Hay Whitney, the financier. The company is paid a declining fee over five years for managing the Yale business, on the theory that as time goes on, it will use the Yale endowment and its prestigious board of directors to build business of its own, either by getting other wealthy clients or by starting a mutual fund. Unlike the Harvard arrangement, however, Yale comes first in buying and selling stocks; the other customers, second.

As John E. Ecklund, Yale's treasurer, described the idea in his 1967 report:

"During the summer of 1967 Yale considered the details of a new organization. In the discussions an approach to the question of incentive developed. Yale would organize a new investment management firm. The firm would advise Yale's endowment. Yale would have priority over all other clients, with their consent, unless a publicly held mutual fund were advised, in which case the priority of Yale would be pro rata according to the size of the funds. Yale would be closely concerned with and informed about the firm's management. The firm would also have other clients and would try to make a profit as a well-run investment management firm. In time it might diversify its activities. In this way, if successful, it could grow to an optimum size in people, equipment and other management resources. From all this Yale could hope to benefit, not only in terms of better management of its own funds, but also in terms of profits from the activities of the firm. The three principal managers of the firm, together with others who might join them from time to time, would, by stock ownership, have a chance to share in the results of its success. On top of this there would be for them the challenge of doing something important for Yale and for education.

"It is obvious that public knowledge that the firm is associated with Yale is likely to help the firm, particularly at the start. This is not objectionable from Yale's point of view—what helps the firm helps Yale. But the firm itself must not, and will not, trade on its connection with Yale. The firm has completed its registration as Investment Counsel, and is ready to talk to others who may be interested in the firm's services. Its clientele, of course, must always be appropriate to its situation."

Shortly after the company was formed, it filed a registration statement for an initial offering of $35 million in stock for a mutual fund to be called Omega Fund. Endowment Management & Research manages its affairs and controls its board of directors, on which Dilworth also sits. Carl Kaysen, director of the Institution for Advanced Study at Princeton, is a director (at an annual fee of about $6,500).

Contrary to what Ecklund says in his report, Omega Fund must openly trade on its Yale connections, for after all, what other reason would there be to purchase a share?

The Wisconsin Alumni Research Foundation got into the investments business from another way around. This organization was established at the University of Wisconsin in Madison in 1925 to exploit the patents to a revolutionary process for synthesizing vitamin D invented by Dr. Harry Steenbock, of the university. Its main function was to keep a lookout for useful inventions in the University of Wisconsin labs. It would take these raw inventions, put in the development work to bring them to the point for commercial use and then license them. Royalties were invested, and from the income the lab recovered costs, paid the inventor his 15 percent share and donated the rest to the university, mostly for building new science laboratories. While WARF won't disclose the size or content of the investment portfolio, it produces about $2 to $3 million a year in income for the university.

The Steenbock patents put WARF into a ticklish situation with the government. In 1943 the government intervened in a patent case between the foundation and a drug concern. In the subsequent court proceedings, WARF admitted that in licensing certain domestic drug companies to make the Vitamin D process, the foundation established minimum prices at which the process could be sold. Moreover, the government accused WARF of conspiring to divide the world markets by licensing the Vitamin D process to various foreign companies, which, according to the government, "have agreed not to import Vitamin D products into the U.S., and plaintiff (WARF) has agreed not to export, and to prohibit its licensees from exporting, Vitamin D products to these foreign countries in which the foreign corporations sell such products. In 1946 WARF surrendered the patents to the Steenbock process to the public domain. By that time, the foundation had realized $8.5 million in royalties from the Vitamin D synthesis. Since then WARF has broadened its operations. "Warfarin" is among the leading rat poisons in the country; it produced $3 million in royalties before the patents gave out. When it is combined with sodium, "Warfarin" becomes an anticoagulant that can be taken orally by humans and is helpful in alleviating blood clotting. This got WARF actively into the drug business. The foundation had also hoped to market a DDT additive that was meant to make the pesticide more effective when bugs had built up resistance to it, but Rachel Carson soured the market for that. The foundation now has a couple of other patents in the works: a fish toxicant that can be used in catfish ponds to kill trash fish; and a new and quicker way to coat pharmacological tablets. But in general, the future for patents looks bleak, since the government is slowly requiring that more and more they be placed in the public domain, thereby limiting the possibility of exploiting them as WARF has done in the past. WARF is also involved in the real estate business, owning three subsidiary companies which operate an amusement-park-type operation at the Wisconsin Dells. And the foundation owns buildings in Madison and Rhinelander, Wisconsin, and runs its own laboratory which makes vitamin concentrates. (The IRS may require this to be spun-off.) Thus in a small way it already is an investment company.

Since WARF publishes no annual reports, one of its advantages is that nobody knows much about its activities outside the patents field. The foundation is already pretty spread out, but it is now thinking of widening its already broad activities. For one thing, it might, as a "public service," move into areas which are too controversial for other manufacturers, and perhaps make, say, a rodenticide for sale. Or acting as a small business investment company, it may begin to finance the early stages of a new business enterprise—perhaps a university spin-off—pulling out once the company was on its feet, thus providing a source of risk capital. This would be especially suitable because WARF has experience in building raw inventions into marketable products, and could provide the advice and contacts necessary to get the naïve professorial entrepreneur off the ground.

If as in these three instances the university perceives itself as an investment trust, it could well go another step and try to influence the growth of new industries. The University of Texas provides an example of how this could come about. Dr. George Kozmetsky is the dean of the College of Business Administration there. He went through the Harvard Business School, taught at Carnegie Tech and was one of the founders of Teledyne, a highly successful electronics company. Kozmetsky is an ambitious supertechnocrat. The business school at the University of Texas does all the usual things; the professors stick around on Saturdays and after hours on week nights to help local businessmen work out management problems, and they go out to the oil country to work with businessmen there. The King Ranch, which finances a chair at the college, had the college make a study of the beef industry, a typical request and one which, while it may not interest the professors particularly, they can scarcely refuse.

But Kozmetsky's real interest lies in projecting what management techniques will be like for the next fifty years. He points out that nobody really knows much about running the new organizations that are taking shape. Corporation executives will have to pull together the efforts of supervisors in widely divergent fields, from social science to accounting. Kozmetsky believes there is little insight to be gotten by employing the staid techniques of making a study, then publishing it. Rather, he feels one needs to perform research, then subject it to a test by running it through a "validation block," then publish the results, and finally start off again on more research. The validation block needs to be a laboratory which is the "real world." One of Kozmetsky's basic interests is "How do you grow a new industry?"

In the middle 1800's, before Texas became a state, the legislature nearly gave the university two million acres of rich farmlands that would produce the income to finance the university's activity; but as it turned out, realistic politics prevailed, and the legislators didn't want to give away all the good farm soil for education. Instead they turned over to the university what was then arid land nobody cared about. Oil was discovered, and this land now produces funds worth $500 million. The money in the fund is restricted in use, but in recent years the university got the state legislature to let it move into the mortgage business, and the University of Texas now supplies mortgage money for housing in the well-to-do sections of Dallas, Fort Worth, San Antonio, Austin and Houston. In addition, the university recently let its first leases for sulphur. Kozmetsky also wants to develop potash on the land, and he believes there are ways to harness solar energy. At the same time he would like to see the money in this fund freed for an investment in developing a marine sciences industry in Texas, and he has pulled together groups of businessmen, scientists and state officials to see whether or not this could be done. Essentially this would involve a consortium among private companies, the university and the state of Texas. The possibilities of the marine science business are enormous, involving the use of submarines for oil drilling and transport, undersea berths for the submarine tankers, recovery of minerals from the ocean depths, dredging out sand and gravel deposits which form at the mouths of estuaries, seafood control and production, harnessing tidal currents for the production of electricity, etc. In Texas the possibilities are especially interesting since the southern coastal areas are little developed and offer the opportunity for building new towns. Some of this land is owned by the King Ranch, whose managers are close to the university, and looking for ways to diversify.

There are other instances where universities are partners with industry in arrangements similar to Kozmetsky's. The University of California through its Irvine campus has helped the Irvine Company start a new city in Orange County, south of Los Angeles. The University of Minnesota got a grant from the Department of Housing and Urban Development to plan and develop a new city in the upper Middle West. The University of Pennsylvania has joined with several other universities around Philadelphia in an urban renewal program, part of which is aimed at replacing black slums with a research park meant for the use of companies interested in medical research, especially the development of medical electronics. It is hoped these companies will be drawn into Philadelphia because of the progressive hospitals connected to the University of Pennsylvania, and as an added lure, the Food and Drug Administration has agreed to construct a regional laboratory within the park. Meanwhile the area universities have jointly formed a University City Science Center, a nonprofit research and marketing organization. Private companies will be able to hire professors for applied research through the institute, and its creation will take the University of Pennsylvania off the hook by providing a nearby place for professors to undertake classified research. (Students and some faculty have protested this activity.) In addition, the center is supposed to promote the urban renewal tract. The plan is modeled along the lines of the Stanford Research Institute and its surrounding industrial park. The scheme has the strong support of Philadelphia, a withering industrial center, which wants very much to consider its universities as a major source of industry for the future.

Universities as institutions and professors as individuals can increase their political power by the way in which they use their expertise in various areas in making deals with business. The computer business shows how this works out, and suggests how universities can adjust to different sorts of roles as a business partner. The International Business Machines Corporation dominates the computer industry, selling more than 80 percent of the computers. This is a large business; computers in operation around the country are judged to be worth $7.2 billion, and the market increases by 25 percent every year. IBM achieved its supremacy by creating a market through shrewd and far-sighted techniques. One of these was to ensure that college students, the future users and buyers of computers, learned about the machines on IBM equipment. Nearly 200,000 college graduates are required to operate the machinery, and if they all learned about them on IBM equipment, their employers might very well find it simpler and less expensive to buy the IBM hardware rather than teach these technicians on another company's equipment. During the past twenty years IBM has made large discounts on equipment to universities, which helped to accomplish this end. It also screwed down another expanding market, the universities themselves. They increasingly use computers for planning, administration and teaching as well as for research, and own computers worth about $160 million; the market expands by nearly half again as much each year.

By making research grants and offering the machinery itself at large discounts, the company gets "free science" in the sense that the professors develop their projects on IBM machines, and these may eventually result in new products or new uses for the machinery, which in all likelihood will result in further extending IBM's share of the market.

IBM tied up the major universities on both East and West Coasts in an ingenious way. At UCLA in 1956 it established an organization called the Western Data Processing Center, which was a dual operation between IBM and UCLA. IBM built the building that houses the computers, provided the machines, serviced them free and shared operating costs with UCLA. IBM used half the computing time, and the other half was utilized without charge by UCLA and over a hundred other participating institutions. They paid only for wire transmission cost if the terminal facilities were on the campus, or for mailing the programs and data. IBM maintained a sales office upstairs at Western Data Processing, and it gave research scholarships to bright students at UCLA to help them in pursuing research on the computers. Some of these IBM research assistants helped instruct other users of the Western Data Processing net how to run machines and cope with the complicated computer languages. Both the Ford Foundation and the Pentagon's Advanced Research Projects Agency helped support the center's work. Thus for the past ten years the University of California acted as a salesman and training school for IBM equipment in the West. One of the clearest results of this arrangement is reflected in the number of computers in use at colleges and universities in California. The number increased by more than one third between 1963 and 1965, and totals about 100, far more than any other state.

In April of 1967 IBM abruptly pulled out of Western Data Processing. The center was renamed the Campus Computing Network, and rather than carry on with the former partnership, the company made a grant of up to $5 million for UCLA computers over a five-year period. IBM left Western Data Processing about the time the Justice Department began antitrust inquiries into the company's operations. One of the areas of concern was understood to be IBM's university operations.

In the East, IBM arranged a similar deal with MIT beginning in 1957. The company provided machinery, services and staff for the institute's computation center. The time on the machines was divided three ways, among IBM, MIT and a network of colleges and universities in the New England area. In 1966, IBM stopped using the computation center. According to MIT, the company never got any exclusive licenses to new inventions from this arrangement.

Nonetheless, until 1962 MIT and IBM enjoyed a very close relationship. Dr. Killian sat on IBM's board of directors, and Thomas J. Watson, Jr., sat on MIT's board of trustees. In 1962, however, both men resigned from one another's boards because of a dispute between MIT and IBM over control of a patent to the memory core unit, a key part of the computer. An MIT professor, Jay W. Forrester, filed a patent to this invention in 1956. He was subsequently challenged by a scientist who worked for RCA. After a complicated legal battle involving MIT on one side, and IBM and RCA on the other, the matter was resolved through consent decrees. In essence, RCA won royalty-free rights to use the invention; MIT gave IBM a license to use the money core unit for $13 million. Forrester's share of the royalties was not disclosed.

IBM has maintained other unusual arrangements with universities. For instance, in 1962 Stanford University purchased at a 60 percent discount an IBM 7090 computer system. After this machinery was installed IBM formed a development laboratory in nearby Palo Alto. Since this laboratory needed computer time, IBM bought back idle time on the machinery it already had sold Stanford at a discount, thus, in effect, subsidizing Stanford two ways. It was well worth IBM's while to ingratiate itself with a university like Stanford, for it is deeply involved in advanced electronic research. This arrangement was broken off in January of 1968, and more recently IBM made a grant of $100,000 to the university for its computer operations.

(In June of 1968, IBM described its current discount policy as follows: "Generally, the present educational allowance for colleges and universities ranges from 10 to 30 percent depending on the equipment. This program is applied uniformly for all educational institutions of this type.")

IBM's dealings with the universities is generally regarded as a great boon for education; without the company's far-sighted help, they never would have been able to afford computers. On the other hand, however, through their liaison with the company the universities assisted in reinforcing IBM's monopoly in the computer business, and provided it with a monopoly in computer science as well.

With the emergence of the so-called "knowledge" industry in the middle 1960's universities and professors began to play an important role in structuring the new education business—one that promises over the long run to be among the giants of American industry. This was accomplished through a series of mergers, the most important of which occurred among the large electronics concerns and publishing companies. Along the way, the electronics companies purchased smaller firms which designed tests, made programmed instructional materials and produced educational toys and cheap scientific instruments.

The leaders are well known. They include IBM and its subsidiary, Science Research Associates; RCA and Random House; Raytheon and D. C. Heath; CBS and Holt, Rinehart & Winston, Inc.; a net of educational companies acquired by Xerox; and the joint ventures of General Electric and *Time*. *Time* later bought the publishing house of Little, Brown.

At first this business was helped by the government, which provided funds from Office of Education, the poverty program and the Defense Department so that ideas and products could be tested. The philosophy that governed its overall development came from the Defense Department and, in particular, from the systems analysts around Secretary McNamara, who sought to persuade both government and industry that the systems approach is the best way to tackle the problems of the Great Society. Consequently, the education-businessmen looked at their job as one of designing and carrying through several functions; that is, initially they wanted to design a school system, provide it with innovative materials and equipment, train the teachers how to use the equipment and then test the finished product—in this case, the student as he comes out of one system and enters another.

(Systems analysis has ramifications beyond education. For instance, General Electric announced it would enter the construction business, erect several new cities in America, presumably provide electricity from a nuclear reactor, make small electric cars, sell the electricity for appliances and heat—all in addition to designing and running the educational system.)

The long-range thrust is toward making the computer into an effective teaching machine. If this can be done, the present school structure as we now know it radically will change and, conceivably, might disappear altogether. Computer-assisted instruction is expensive, and its development depends on government financing. This has been held up because of the Vietnam war, and because most of the companies that jumped into the business either were unable or unwilling to engage in the long-range sophisticated marketing procedures necessary to pull it off. Thus Xerox lost some of its most intelligent and interesting employees because it insisted on selling education as it might one of its machines. The GE-*Time* combine, which at this writing is still headed by Francis Keppel, the former director of the Office of Education, was torn by internal strife, with large numbers of the GE personnel, who were mostly hardware specialists, leaving the company.

The electronics companies have found they can make money simply by running the publishing companies as profitable subsidiaries, continuing to churn out traditional and tedious textbooks which produce more money for more acquisitions rather than meshing activities of subsidiaries. The systems approach has turned out to be little more than a publicity screen behind which the country once again watches holding companies build.

While companies without sophisticated notions of market manipulations won't make it, the possibilities for this industry are enormous over the long run. Already, however, the industry lines are taking shape, and markets are being carved out as the government looks on. The future depends on long-term investments in research, and it shows perhaps best of all a university-industrial consortium in operation. For in many respects the key to the direction and shape of the industry lies with a very small group of university scientists.

There are two main ways of using the computer in education. It may be thought of as a kind of mechanical teacher. Here the possibilities are limitless. As the child sits at the typewriter and begins the dialogue with his computor-tutor, the machine will sense out his weaknesses and provide him with remedies. Instruction will be tailored to each individual. There will be no classes, nor, for that matter, any need for schools. The student can sit at home. In the morning he will dial into the computer and ask for French. After half an hour of this he can switch to the library (all the books are stored in computers) and get the machine to print out parts of *Paradise Lost,* which he will study and then answer some questions the computer puts to him about the poem. Once a semester a student can go along to a learning center to meet with discussion groups and to chat with his counselor. The counselor already will have asked the computer for an audit on the student, and will be prepared to discuss his progress and qualifications for jobs. It will be interesting to compare the student's actual progress with the computer's predictions of his progress, which in most cases will have turned out to be all too accurate.

The Californians are especially enthusiastic about the possibilities here. Dr. Robert Tschirgi, dean of planning for the University of California, feels computers can help universities get on with their real job. The primary business of any university, he says, is the creation, storage, manipulation and dissemination of information. Once all the libraries at universities are hooked together through computer systems, there will at last be the "great composite university which is truly universal." To those who are frightened of machines, Dr. Tschirgi has these words of encouragement: "A book is an inanimate, unresponsive friend at best, yet love and attachment are well-recognized emotions to be displayed toward books. Why should it be surprising, therefore, that a reactive, facile, responsive computer may also generate a form of affection in its human users? Is it any less comprehensible to imagine a generation with nostalgic memories of one's old computer-tutor than to have cherished remembrances of ivy-colored walls?"

Ralph W. Gerard, dean of the graduate division at the University of California at Irvine, is also keen for the machines, and through his leadership Irvine has got a reputation as a center for computer-assisted instruction. Gerard flies around the country proselytizing for computers. In his writings he described the Irvine plan: "The campus became interested in the possibility of really interweaving these two great information-handling systems. A university is primarily a system for storing, retrieving, processing, disseminating and creating information (research which creates information being less present in lower institutions); and computers do exactly the same, even creating information in the sense that mathematics, though a tautology, creates usable information by manipulating existing knowledge and assumptions. Clearly they are made for each other and our hope was to build a total system for information handling by combining the resources of both. We set up, for example, a computer 'facility' rather than a computer 'center,' to imply an interpenetration rather than a boundary . . .

"I like to think of the total system as a sort of sandwich," Gerard continued, "of data bank on the one side and users on the other, interacting via the information-processing apparatus."

Gerard and Tschirgi are computer fetishists who insist information is knowledge, and that the function of a university is to provide information.

In 1963 and 1964 Chancellor Daniel G. Aldrich, Jr., at Irvine, and Gerard got IBM interested in setting up programs there. The company agreed to install a 1400 system and to supply staff and engineers. An IBM employee, Dr. J. A. Kearns, came along to head the project and was given a part-time appointment to the Graduate School of Administration. The idea was to see whether the computer could be used as a library, for various administrative functions and for teaching.

Gerard paints a glowing picture. He says that one half of all the students on the Irvine campus spend at least one hour a week on the computer, and that computers are used in teaching biology, mathematics, economics, sociology and psychology.

After speaking with Gerard, I went along to see the computer in action, and ran into a senior staff man who told me in a jaundiced manner that it wasn't operating because they couldn't make the new IBM 360 system work right. This gentleman was exceedingly glum about the possibilities of very many students learning much of anything on the Irvine computers. So was the dean of Social Sciences, James G. March. When I asked him about the use of the machine to teach sociology, he replied grimly that all the computer did was to print out some basic definitions in an introductory course, which, as he pointed out, one could get just as well from reading a book. He went on to say that a minute portion of any introductory course was on a computer, that students spent little time on them, and that most of the time was taken up programming them. March said the difficulty was to devise a system which could answer questions rather than ask them. The most one could really expect was to have a machine pose a problem to the student, who could then go ahead and answer it on his own.

At Irvine, however, IBM put in $1.5 million over a two-year period, and what it was getting in exchange was free science—in the sense that the university people would be developing programs on the company's machines—and, perhaps best of all, publicity through Gerard. An IBM supervisor had infiltrated the faculty, and, in fact, as a professor had assumed control of a research station, complete with the dean of the Graduate School as a mouth organ.

At Stanford University in Palo Alto, first IBM and

then RCA settled down around Patrick Suppes, a professor at the university, who is widely acknowledged to be one of the main hopes for computer-assisted instruction. With IBM equipment, and with money from the Office of Education, Suppes set up a special program at the Brentwood elementary schools where children come in and sit before a computer console. The computer asks them to choose among objects shown on a television-type screen, and in selecting the answer, the child touches the proper column on the screen with an instrument called a light pen. Depending on whether his answer is right or wrong, the child advances to the next problem.

For RCA, Suppes has made a drill-and-practice routine for first-grade reading and second-grade math which is shown over computer consoles at different Palo Alto grade schools as well as in New York City. RCA built a computer in Palo Alto to service much of the country because Suppes and his people were close by. Suppes works on a nonexclusive basis as a consultant for RCA and develops materials for IBM.

All of this leaves Suppes and his staff in an enviable position; in a very real way a university professor is helping to structure an industry.

The much more obvious and simple way to use computers is as an extension of the intelligence to aid in solving tedious or complicated problems, much in the manner that one might use an automobile or a steam engine. This necessitates a simple method for unsophisticated people to talk to the machine. This kind of work goes forward all over the country, but one of the most interesting projects is at Dartmouth, where the college is made a consortium with the General Electric Company.

During the early 1960's John G. Kemeny and several others at Dartmouth wanted to know more about what a computer was and how it worked. At the time, however, computers were expensive. Kemeny got a grant from the National Science Foundation, and with the help of twelve Dartmouth undergraduates, set about designing a computer system, eventually making one that utilized two machines. One of them posed the problem. The other was a sort of switching device the operator talked into; the machine would then send along instructions to the computer about what problems to solve, in the meantime keeping the operator posted on what was happening. This saved a lot of time, and is known in the business as "time-sharing."

General Electric made a switching machine which Kemeny liked, and while the company had never thought of putting it to work as part of a computer, GE agreed to let Dartmouth have it at a 40 percent educational discount. Kemeny and the Dartmouth students finished their computer in the fall of 1964. A year later GE got interested in the possibilities of the Dartmouth time-share model, and set out to duplicate it. But this wasn't so easy, since GE used equipment that was a little different from that initially used in the Dartmouth system, and that system didn't work. Fortunately, this was over a Christmas vacation and three Dartmouth undergraduates were flown out to Arizona, where the GE executives were nervously biting their nails in anticipation of a formal presentation to the chief officers of the company. The Dartmouth boys got it going, and GE eventually put the system into operation; by 1967 there were fifteen of them around the country, all oversubscribed.

Dartmouth then wanted to move on and try its hand at designing a much larger system, one that would hook together twelve colleges and twenty high schools. The early negotiations were complicated, but despite Kemeny's success with GE, the company was sluggish about taking up the new scheme. After these discussions had dragged on for some time, the dean of Dartmouth's Engineering School, Myron Tribus, intervened on behalf of Kemeny. Tribus was a consultant to GE, and almost at once the negotiations moved to a higher level where a deal was hammered out. Tribus stated that when it came to discussing which company's machinery was to be used, he quit as a GE consultant so as to avoid any possible suggestion of conflict of interest. In the final arrangements, GE agreed to give Dartmouth a $2.5 million computer. In return Dartmouth will help to develop the hardware system and write the programs to be used on it. Some of the work is to be a joint venture between Dartmouth and GE. Out of this deal, Dartmouth gets the machine and is featured in GE advertising. For its part, GE gets worldwide rights to whatever programs Kemeny's group makes, as well as rights to inventions coming from joint ventures between the college and the company, and it keeps half the time on the machine so it can use it for demonstrating Kemeny's work to potential customers.

4. The Proprietors

In recent years professors have started a number of new kinds of companies involved in "social problem solving." The theory is that the techniques of systems analysis employed in making complicated missile and defense systems can be used to solve various political problems as well—in other words, that the engineers and scientists who figured out how to send a rocket to the moon, could also figure out how to build a fine school system or end poverty.

This is all very vague, but what the companies usually have in mind is the collection of different sorts of data, which can be assembled and built into a model that will simulate, or imitate, human activity. If one could quantify human activity, they argue, one might also be able to predict and control it. Thus, what the companies offer for sale are various technological techniques, which more nearly resemble propaganda processes, owned by the client when the work is complete. The propaganda process usually needs to include an intelligence system, and it must adhere to the dictates of the technological organizations, which is to say it must above all appear to be efficient even when it is not. The interesting possibility that human behavior can be controlled has led to a virtual movement among the social scientists around the country who collect all sorts of data in hopes that these "social indicators" may lead to such a system.

The proprietors of the social-problem-solving companies spring quite naturally from the elitist world of the university. Certainly part of the idea behind the business is to transfer the attitudes and styles of university life to the rest of society so that the corporation executive or government official may bully his subordinates the way Dr. Pusey does his students. Taken seriously, these entrepreneurs are a profoundly anti-democratic lot. However, as individuals they are inclined to be eccentric, lively and amusing people; it never is altogether clear whether they know what they are doing, or indeed, whether they take themselves especially seriously.

Simulmatics Corporation was among the earliest of the simulation companies, with a special interest in political propaganda. The company was organized in 1959 by Edward L. Greenfield, a public relations man, and three professors—Ithiel de Sola Pool of MIT, William N. McPhee of Columbia, Robert P. Abelson from Yale. They had devised a mathematical model of the political behavior of the American electorate, and persuaded several wealthy liberals to finance the project with an eye to providing the Kennedy organization with specific information on voting patterns so that John Kennedy might make the right moves to counter Nixon. This polling method, for example, showed that women leaned toward Nixon because they felt he could handle delicate matters of foreign policy better than Kennedy. To counter this, Simulmatics suggested Kennedy debate Nixon on television. The Simulmatics predictions turned out to be accurate, and trading on this success, the company went on to other work.

In general, Simulmatics engages principally "in estimating possible human behavior by the use of computer technology," and this led it to make models of the Venezuelan economy for AID, and to draw up a computer program called Dynamark, which can "assess brand loyalty" by evaluating results of the test-marketing of different products. It gained considerable publicity by advertising and producing educational games. The most popular is one for youngsters called the Life Career Game. Students are divided up into teams of two or three people. Each team is assigned a fictitious student, and the idea is to plan a worthwhile life for this hypothetical person, thereby helping to instruct the youngsters in how to make the most advantageous and efficient use of their youth. In the Legislative Game, sometimes called the Direct Democracy Game, players pretend to be congressmen. They are provided with cards that will tell how the people back home vote. Then they simulate congressmen at work. This game calls for sessions in a cloakroom where the players can swindle one another, and they have a chance to act out the less meaningful forms of parliamentary procedure on the floor of Congress.

Simulmatics is obviously meant as a convenience for its professor officers and directors. The education games were designed by a group of professors at Johns Hopkins headed by James Coleman, then marketed through Simulmatics, where Coleman is a vice-president and director. Simulmatics has purchased polling data from the Furst Survey Research Center, Incorporated, which is owned by Sidney Furst, who was then a vice-president and director of Simulmatics. (He is no longer an officer or director of Simulmatics.) Simulmatics hired its own vice-president, Professor McPhee, as a consultant, through Columbia University's Bureau of Applied Social Research, where he was employed.

Educational games are only a small part of Simulmatics' activities, and the main work of the company seems to reflect the interests of Pool, who next to Greenfield holds the most stock (50,000 shares). Pool is a professor and chairman of the political science section at MIT, and director of the research program for international communication at the Center for International Studies. (The center was originally financed by the CIA, and Pool sometimes consults for the agency.) Pool is mainly concerned with propaganda studies; at MIT he studies mass media propaganda techniques in Communist countries; on the side and in the summer he is actively engaged through Simulmatics in conducting secret research in South Vietnam for the Pentagon's Advanced Research Projects Agency. While neither Pool nor anybody else at Simulmatics will talk about this work, the contracts ran close to $700,000 in 1967 and accounted for three quarters of the firm's business. (In 1967 it grossed just over $1 million.) Simulmatics maintains a villa in Saigon, and flies out graduate students and professors from Harvard, MIT and other universities. (Arthur Smithies, the Harvard economist, made a trip to Vietnam.) They interviewed Vietcong defectors and prisoners, and sampled other groups among the South Vietnamese population, with the hope of figuring out a pacification program. In addition to his stockholding, the prospectus says Pool gets a minimum consultant fee from the company of $5000 a year, plus $100 per day in certain circumstances.

While Simulmatics continues to ballyhoo the public opinion polls it conducted in 1960 for Kennedy, the Democrats were not sufficiently interested in 1964 to hire them. Simulmatics tried to get into the poverty program by designing a community-action program which it intended to set up at some undisclosed site, but was turned down by the Office of Economic Opportunity. Subsequent to their departure from the government, Daniel P. Moynihan, former Assistant Secretary of Labor, and Adam Yarmolinsky, one of McNamara's aides, both professors at Harvard, were added to the research board, and this was a shot in the arm. Eastman Kodak asked Moynihan in to mediate the dispute it was having with a militant black group in Rochester. This resulted in an extended consulting arrangement, which Moynihan ran through Simulmatics, and he brought along Yarmolinsky to carry out some of the work.

In fact, Simulmatics looks like nothing more than a dummy corporation through which Pool runs his outside Defense work. There isn't anything unusual in this. Many professors set up companies as fronts for consulting, especially in controversial areas. One of the better known of these firms is Mathematica in Princeton. Oscar Morgenstern, the econometrician and inventor of games theory, is chairman and the company is often viewed as a dummy to serve Morganstern and a group of other Princeton professors who want to do outside consulting. The firm put out a lavish brochure with four pages of photographs of the various Princeton professors whose services were offered. But the university cracked down and made them stop trading so blatantly on Princeton's name.

Clark Abt, who is president of Abt Associates, Incorporated, is an admirer of Pool's but his company is more varied in its activities. Abt, who is in his late thirties, graduated from Johns Hopkins, then got a Ph.D. at MIT and went to work for Raytheon, where he became manager of the Advanced Systems Department. Abt floats easily in the Cambridge intellectual pond, and teaches an honors seminar at Harvard. At MIT and Raytheon, his main interest was in working out some computer simulations to solve the arms-control dilemma. In the mid-1960s Thomas Schelling, the Harvard professor who runs an arms-control seminar for the Cambridge intellectuals, put Abt on to a contract with Educational Services, Incorporated, another joint Harvard-MIT undertaking. It designs new curricula for schools. Here was a chance to apply simulation theories by working on an educational game. It was a small contract, but it helped start Abt in business. This was not especially fortunate as it turned out, since Abt made such a mess of the game it had to be done all over again. Abt Associates began in 1965 in a warehouse attic with a handful of people and a small contract. It now has a staff of 120, some sixty-five consultants from Harvard and MIT, and grosses about $2 million a year. Abt, like Simulmatics, survived by first working for the military, making counterinsurgency games, which were then used as training devices. One of the more popular games, called Agile-Coin (Coin means counterinsurgency), sought to simulate the principal aspects of the terror phase of internal revolutionary conflict in a Southeast Asia setting. The introduction to Agile-Coin helps explain what Abt set out to do: "If the problems of counterinsurgency could be described in terms of a small number of variables, like most physical processes, mathematical analysis could soon solve them. If the state of social science knowledge were comparable to that of physical sciences, in which most important variables and relationships can be defined quantitatively, direct mathematical analysis would possibly be more attractive than simulation.

"The situation now is that we must deal as best we can with a complex problem that has not been described in quantitative form. Simulation is one way of moving from the qualitative to quantitative and from subjective impressions to objective analysis, theory building, experiment, theory correction, prediction and control. And that is the final objective of our applied research—control of insurgencies."

In Agile-Coin, actors represent insurgents, government forces and villagers. The insurgents and government forces are meant to knock each other off, at the same time gaining the loyalty of as many villagers as possible. For their part, the villagers try to keep losses down, stop the conflict as soon as possible and end on the winning side. The game is played with the actors in different rooms, or in an outdoor version, tents can be used. Abt worked up another version of this game, called Urb-Coin, to depict urban counterinsurgency, and found that children in the Boston slums were enthusiastic about playing it.

Abt does not care to be too closely associated with the fad in games, and he is equally interested in running schools and Job Corps camps. The company makes scenarios to show how different countries will line up in future power struggles; works on curricula for Creative

Playthings, a CBS subsidiary; and creates complicated cost-effectiveness models for different government agencies. Abt has consciously moved away from the military work into other areas.

The company does its selling casually. It demonstrated Agile-Coin for thirty-five government employees, and this eventually led to a $50,000 contract for the Bureau of Standards for a game to help explain some of the complicated economic and political interests that influence development of a new transportation policy for the Northeast Corridor (Boston to Washington, D.C.).

Richard H. Rosen, the senior operations analyst at Abt, described how the game works: eighty actors, representing different economic and political interests, play for two days at simulating the economy and politics of the Northeast Corridor. The objective of each actor is to come up with a plan that will benefit his interests. Nine rooms are required for play, three of them for negotiating.

Control has representatives in each room and they try to keep the game moving along. Thirty actors represent various business interests, such as the New York textile industry, the Providence jewelers, Connecticut and Massachusetts toolmakers, etc. The communications-industry actor is made up to resemble the late Henry Luce. The economic actors lead off in the game as they might in the "real world," by placing orders for raw materials and specifying how the goods are to be shipped. As the economic actors go through the motions of buying, manufacturing and shipping goods in the Northeast Corridor, the data are run through a computer, and begin to show the transportation system bogging down. Each round of the game lasts about forty minutes, but with the help of the computer, the forty minutes simulate a year's time (the game represents what happens between 1960 and 1980).

The economic actors get more and more frustrated as the computer shows them losing increasing amounts of money because of late or lost shipments. The businessmen actors look around for politicians to fix things up. Now the political actors, who have been sitting on the sidelines, begin to play. They represent all sorts of elected officials—senators, congressmen, mayors, heads of state legislatures—as well as representatives from political pressure groups, trade associations, conservation societies, state and local planning agencies. There is even a team of actors representing federal bureaucrats who squabble over who gets to do what.

Each person is equipped with a scenario of his role, telling him how he might act in real life; otherwise, the play is free, and as Rosen says, "The actors can negotiate, lie, steal, cheat, anything, so long as it's in concert with their objective, which is to make a transportation plan that satisfies their own needs."

After five or six rounds of wheeling-dealing, the federal government calls a conference and presents a plan, which in the test play was hooted down. (This is real enough, since the appearance of the "feds" on the local scene almost invariably arouses hostility among the local people, who resent being pushed around by the Washington bureaucrats.) More conferences follow, with state and local governments and other interested parties presenting different plans. The haggling drags on; under the game rules, a new plan must be agreed upon by the end of the first day of play. Rosen points out that in the "real world" one way to get political agreement is to wear down the participants. Thus, in the transportation game, the actors must continue playing into the wee hours of the morning until they agree on a plan. This, says Rosen, "is a real simulation of reality." During the second day of the game the computer is used to break down the general plan into details, and then it simulates the new system. The players watch to see how well it works.

The transportation game can be broken down to deal with regional problems. In one test play involving the states of Connecticut and Rhode Island, actors hammered out an interstate transportation plan. Basically, the prob-

lem was how to get workers in Providence to jobs in
Hartford. The participants agreed to build a high-speed
rapid-transit system from Hartford to Providence as well
as a fast highway between the two cities. These measures
would facilitate transportation of both people and goods.
In addition, it was agreed that Connecticut should enlarge
the Hartford airfield into an international airport, and a
high-speed subway should be run from the center of town
out to the airport. (The subway could interconnect with
rapid-transit systems coming up from New York and
down from Boston.) To pay for much of this, Connecticut decided to float a bond issue. This was feasible because the actors representing United Aircraft, based in
Hartford, agreed to buy the bonds, which offered a good
yield. In addition, United, which makes aircraft engines
as well as high-speed railway equipment, stood to profit
from the increased business. Rhode Island got some federal money to develop the Providence harbor, and more
important, Connecticut promised not to develop the harbors of New London, which might have competed with
Providence. Thus, Connecticut traded Rhode Island the
rights to build a major seaport in exchange for a big air
center.

The company sought to heighten the reality of this
game by persuading senators and congressmen to simulate themselves, but in the end, had to settle for the members' legislative assistants. Since these gentlemen spent
most of the time, in effect, simulating their employers
anyhow, Abt produced the effect of simulating a simulation of a simulation. This phenomenon pleased the people
at Abt, although its meaning was not entirely clear.

Abt believes in profit, which is part of the "reward system," and he says at the same time that this company is
"apolitical." Then he remembers the time one of the staff
did some after-hours campaigning for right-wing candidates which didn't help the firm's image. They fired him.
Abt is enthusiastic about peer teaching, either among little children or in a Job Corps camp for teen-age girls.

This is innovating and exciting; then he adds, it is also cheaper.

While both Simulmatics and Abt Associates operate under the guise of a neutral technology, their politics are really fairly obvious. Simulmatics has been mainly involved in seeking to discover ways of manipulating the South Vietnamese; Abt Associates began by doing pretty much the same thing, working in counterinsurgency, but transferred the counterinsurgency games to school children in the slums of Boston. Simulation companies are not so popular as they once were; their proprietors are often regarded as cultists, and the generals who were persuaded to hire them by the liberals in the Kennedy and early Johnson administrations are sour on the whole business. Counterinsurgency is an unmanly way to fight, and anyhow, it was a dreadful flop in Vietnam.

By far the most energetic operator among the Cambridge intellectuals is J. Sterling Livingston, a professor at the Harvard Business School. Livingston has established half a dozen companies since the end of the second world war. In the Harvard tradition, he, too, is a manipulator, a whiz at wheeling-dealing, and is of current interest because of the form his organizations take. They suggest how professors may be brought more fully into business activity.

During the second world war Livingston ran a purchasing course for the Navy at the Harvard Business School; in the midst of this he was ordered to Washington to help rewrite the then nearly incomprehensible purchasing instructions by which the Navy was supposed to function. Livingston and a group of other officers did the work, simplifying the instructions, and in cases where the procedures became complicated, they would stick in an illustration of how the form was to be filled out. After the war Livingston returned to the Harvard Business School and wrote a thesis on government procurement policies; subsequently, the Navy asked him if he could continue to ad-

vise them on procurement matters. Livingston wanted to
run this business through the school, but the dean didn't
think it was proper, and instead suggested that Livingston
organize a company and perform the work outside. This
led to the creation of Harbridge House Inc., whose sole
business at first consisted of telling the Navy how to improve procurement methods. Harvard and MIT professors were consultants, and one of Livingston's partners
was Paul R. Ignatius, who now is Secretary of the Navy.
Livingston's reputation as a procurement specialist got
around, and the other military services hired Harbridge
House to help them out. During the Korean War the
company was grossing $1.5 million a year. (Meanwhile,
Livingston was still a professor at the Harvard Business
School.) Since they had instructed the services how to
best industry in procurement negotiations, Harbridge
House was next hired by corporations that, in effect,
wanted to find a way to do in the services, and asked
Harbridge House in effect to devise a means of bettering
its own system. By this time (1958) Livingston was getting bored with the work. He quit as president of Harbridge House, selling out his interest for an undisclosed
sum. When he left, the company was grossing $3 million
a year.

Next Livingston ran a course at the Harvard Business
School called Project Management, which was meant to
help the military understand and cope with the complicated business problems involved in building weapons
systems like the Polaris missile. It was clear to Livingston
that the military did not possess the management information required to grapple with the business, so he
started another company called Management Systems
Corporation, which again relied heavily on professors
from Harvard and MIT, as well as some from Stanford.
Management Systems assisted the Navy, Air Force and
NASA in developing ways to keep tabs on weapons and
missile systems, and it too had an annual income of about
$3 million when Livingston tired of the business and

merged it into a new firm called Peat, Marwick, Livingston & Company, which itself was a subsidiary of Peat, Marwick, Mitchell & Company, the large accounting company. Basically, Management Systems got its reputation from writing "do it yourself" manuals for military procurers.

Recently Livingston became enthusiastic about the possibilities in education technology, that is, the use of computers, films, games and other types of media for industrial and government training programs, as well as for more general educational usage. He sold out his interest in Peat, Marwick, Livingston, retaining only a consulting job there, and began a company called Sterling Institute. The institute consists of several centers, which in effect are subsidiary companies that Livingston assembled; the institute maintains offices in Boston, New York and Washington. In Washington it runs a lavish training center, with modernistic classrooms where businessmen and government officials can take special courses. Most of the time is booked by Peat, Marwick, Mitchell. Livingston put together this assortment of companies very much as a new university might assemble a faculty. In almost all the cases, the subsidiaries were previously owned by well-known professors, and by buying out these companies, Livingston was also buying all the free consulting time of the professor, his graduate students and protégés, who came along as staff. Thus he jerry-built a small conglomerate corporation out of university professors. For instance, Livingston took over a company owned by Professor Ed Robinson of Boston University. Robinson was making instructional materials for banks to use in training employees. One of the clients was the New England Merchants Bank, which acted as a marketing agent for Robinson's training materials, selling them to correspondent banks. So by buying Robinson's company and renaming it the Training Development Center, Livingston picked up a professor, a product, a client and a marketing apparatus. Then Livingston took advantage of an internal crisis at the General Learning Corporation, the *Time*-General Electric venture into education. In mid-1967 there was a battle within this firm, with the result that many of the GE people were fired. Livingston went to New York and picked off the likely-looking prospects from the GE discards. In the process he hired Donald Torr, who had not been fired but who had sickened of the internecine warfare. While at General Learning Torr had worked with the Department of the Navy on various projects, and this gave him an inside line on what the Navy was doing in education. As a result of hiring Torr, Sterling Institute bid on a contract to design a course in economics at the Naval Academy at Annapolis, and won, taking down a contract worth nearly $1 million. There are five other centers in the institute, and Livingston runs a hotel in the Virgin Islands as well.

Probably the most interesting of all Livingston's acquisitions was the Human Resources Development Company, a down-in-the-dumps enterprise begun by David C. McClelland, the well-known Harvard psychologist and motivation expert. As in all the other acquisitions, purchasing Human Resources meant buying McClelland, his graduate students and protégés, who came along to become staff members of what was named the Behavorial Science Center. Livingston put money into this operation, brought in some management experts from the Harvard Business School and helped out in marketing. "He gave credibility to our brainstormy ideas," says a center employee. "I think this is what he does a lot. He picks up ideas that are pretty good, you could say half-baked in a way because they're not developed and polished, and helps get them worked out into a program that provides a lot of credibility in selling them."

Thanks to Livingston, the center is now very much on the go. It has developed a motivational leadership course for fraternity men, and is working on a program for naval chaplains ("helping the chaplain make the transition from his role as a pastor to a manager and supervisor"). It has a contract from Massachusetts Mutual Life Insurance Company "to improve the managerial and parental effectiveness" of both agents and their wives. A company official said it was "kind of a challenge."

The U.S. Department of Labor hired the center to make comic books that would motivate blacks to hurry along to the local labor department office and inquire about job training. The center supplied the theme, and the comics were made by American Visuals. They are peopled with characters who look like rather dark models in Jantzen swimsuit ads. And they all speak what McClelland's people must think to be jive talk. One of them, a sharp-looking fellow, is getting out of a new car to shoot the breeze with his old pals at the neighborhood billiard parlor, all of whom are made to appear down and out. As the fellow approaches, he says "POWER IS GREEN BABY!" and then goes on to drive home the point that you can get green power by going to your nearest employment office and getting some skill training. Halfway through, another character asks, "What about prejudice, man? You know what I mean, suppose you're black!" The answer to this is: "THE MAN needs help! You'd be surprised how UNprejudiced he gets when YOU got something his business needs. GREEN IS A POWERFUL COLOR, TOO, BABY!" And then, "MAKE YOUR OWN POWER AND MAKE IT GREEN." On the back cover of the comic is a coupon one is supposed to fill in and take along to the employment office. It is an imitation of a dollar bill with a place for name and address in the middle. Other comics in the series are entitled *How to Use the System to Make It,* and *You Are Nowhere, Baby!* An interesting comic is about a black girl with straight hair (blacks in McClelland's comics have straight hair) who is trying to figure out which man to marry. The comic is called *"The Man for Me?"* Ellie is telling her sister about the man in her life. "But what a drag," says Ellie of Ernie. "He works for a printer . . . Now this course cuts in on our evening."

"So you miss a few evenings a week now," says Sis. "That's better than missing 'em later on! Someday you'll be a mother with a family . . . then he'll be there!"

"Oh, Sis, you talk as if I was going to marry him!"

"And why not? He sure fits the formula for happiness! Smart . . . steady . . . fun . . . earning . . . learning . . . and getting ahead; a future . . . and he likes you. Sounds real solid—a REAL MAN! How lucky can a girl get?"

This hip talk is followed by a check list where the reader can rate the men she knows according to McClelland's motivation theories. If you check the right boxes—"plans for the future, tries to move ahead, helps others, interested in people and his community, etc."—then you're O.K. and are rewarded at the bottom of the page with the statement: "Looks like your best bet. You may have to work at the start until he gets ahead, but the future looks cool!"

In the Washington office, the Behavioral Science Center got together small businessmen from the Washington ghetto and tried to help motivate them to achieve more. Black people in Washington are tired of being studied. However, the Center staff managed to obtain sixty-five persons for a trial. The businessmen play a game, competing against one another to see who can build the most atomic tractors with Tinker toys in a given period of time. If the players do not meet their own production goals, they then must reset them, or perhaps beef up production by subcontracting out to one of the other players. In effect, the game seeks to simulate modern production. The center staff found that black businessmen are hesitant to trust or collaborate with others, so they devised another game, Disarmament, to overcome this. The players are split into two teams, then given weapons cards. They represent two nations with equal weapons, and through the instructor, who operates as the United Nations, they are meant to negotiate for disarmament.

"One of the things we're trying to teach these people, or get them to teach themselves, is that they can reach white standards, not marginally successful black standards," says an official at Sterling Institute.

Another sort of organization is gaining favor among the academics, a modern, free-wheeling Galbraithian enterprise—part think tank, part business company, part university; an organization which is interchangeable with any of the three, called "the floating crap game company." The term originated with OSTI, which means the Organization for Social and Technical Innovation. OSTI is a new, nonprofit organization with headquarters in Cambridge, Massachusetts. The president of OSTI is Donald Schon, who left his job as director of the Institute for Applied Technology at the Bureau of Standards. Schon was tired of the government, and wanted to go back to Arthur D. Little & Company, a research company in Cambridge for which he had previously worked, to start an Institute of Innovation. There he hoped he could try out some of his ideas about social change. But Little didn't want to start an institute and instead loaned Schon $150,000, agreeing to work on joint ventures with him.

Schon says he worked out the idea for starting OSTI during a conference at Woods Hole, Massachusetts, in 1966. This was when government, industry, labor, university people got together, and secretly drew up plans for a government-led consortium modeled along the lines of Comsat, which would build millions of units of low-income housing quickly and cheaply. It was the first major effort by people within the government to form consortia arrangements with industry. Schon's organization reflects the kind of organizational theories in the Comsat proposal. And some of the people who encouraged him then to start the company took a major hand in drafting the proposal. Among them were Hortense Gabel, former rent administrator in New York City, and Ezra Ehrenkrantz, head of Buildings Systems Corporation, both of whom are now connected with OSTI, and who will sometimes hire OSTI, or be hired by it, and Leonard Duhl, the HUD advisor who thought of the "floating crap game" phrase for describing the enterprise.

OSTI has a "core group" of people, and around them "linking members" who sometimes work for OSTI, and sometimes employ OSTI. In addition to Schon, the core group includes Frederick Wiseman, the attorney who made *Titicut Follies,* the film about a Massachusetts mental hospital; Noel Day, a sociologist and a Roxbury community organizer; William B. Drake, an engineer at the University of Michigan, and Stanford Kravitz, who headed the Office of Economic Opportunity's research and demonstration office and now teaches at Brandeis.

In a book called *Technology and Change,* Schon sets out the theory on which OSTI operates. As he sees it, the form of the corporation is changing from a pyramid, with white-collar slaves arranged in spreading layers beneath a boss, into a circular design where different groups of people with their different interests work together but are linked to a central core which provides them with services and a bank for funds, and most important, acts as a broker among the different linking parts in arranging deals and doing jobs.

This is not an unusual idea. The model is repeated with variations in the large conglomerate corporations; multiversities are not unlike it, with graduate institutes and laboratories surrounding the central bank, or administration; and perhaps the most striking similarity is to the design of a computer operation, with the computer clients arranged in a circle around the great machine, all waiting for a crack at its problem-solving abilities. But the crux of Schon's theory is his concept of the management. The leader of this enterprise "works to enable people within the organization to learn to innovate. His vision is of change, learning, innovation from within. He does not attempt to shoulder the burden of converting uncertainty to risk; he attempts to help others learn to do this. He codes, not imposes, his ideas about substantive projects; he does not regard himself as the principal source of ideas. Instead he attempts to build resources for innovation. To the extent that he is manipulative, he manipulates the process by which ideas come into being and turn into reality. He attempts to teach and create models, but on the level of process rather than on specific accomplishment. His assumption is that it is possible, without relaxing standards of performance or deflecting attention from the work at hand, to enable people in the organization to use their own potential for innovation and to set a style in the organization for doing this."

OSTI helped the Harvard Business School train Peace Corps volunteers for life in India by letting them hang around failing small businesses in Roxbury, the black slum of Boston. This was supposed to help them discover what life would be like in India.

OSTI is making curricula for the State University of New York's new Oxbridge-type campus at Old Westbury, New York, where the students will spend most of the year in the Long Island horse country and then go into a city slum for a while to see what life is like there—thereby getting the laboratory experience which white middle-class youth can no longer afford to miss. Or there is another education scheme for the Boston area, whereby students would go to a different kind of school in a different setting each year; thus poor black children could go to school in the well-to-do part of Cambridge for a year, while the smart sons of Harvard professors could go down to Roxbury—a game of changing cages.

OSTI's most interesting experiment is in Roxbury, where it acts as advisor to a community development corporation known as Circle Associates. This was Day's idea. He was sick of poverty programs which never changed the economic base; he was tired of talking about participatory democracy and was down on cooperatives, which he didn't think mattered much. Circle Associates was to be none of these things. It was a group of black businessmen, organized on a purely Stalinist basis, to wring hard deals out of white companies either in or near Roxbury. Its goal was to centralize and collect capital, in effect, buying back the place from the whites; then when that was finished, turn over the organization to the people. OSTI and A. D. Little were helping Circle build a fund of about $500,000 for venture capital. Circle sought vending contracts at factories, and wanted guard and maintenance and catering contracts. This would put people in the community to work. Then with the money from the venture capital fund it would try to start supermarkets, small loan companies and primary manufacturing concerns in such businesses as printing and painting.

In addition to the new companies, there are, of course, rafts of social-problem solvers within graduate schools, institutes and other sections of universities. It should be pointed out in their defense that they claim to be developing options which will permit people a greater scope of action. But this seems to be a hollow argument, for the options reflect the assumptions of the people who create them. And as even a cursory description of the activities of the concerns listed above suggests, these are quite likely to be those of the concerned white humane liberal who would very much like to have everyone live pretty much as he does. Abt, for example, wants to control foreign insurgencies for the benefit of the United States and those within the United States for anyone who hires him. Pool wants to pacify the Vietnamese for us; Livingston's people work to give poor black Americans white middle-class values, and even Schon, by far the most interesting of the lot, sets out to imitate Stalin in behalf of the citizenry of Roxbury.

None of this should seem especially surprising, for after all, while activities of the professors-entrepreneurs are cast in the form of corporations, their values are those of the university, patronizing and authoritarian. The essence of their propaganda is efficiency, the governing myth of American corporate society. Thus they offer for sale different ways of achieving the same thing: a static, boring, consumptive middle class through a constant change of machine parts.

5. Politics

In the spring of 1967 President Johnson named George Baker, Dean of the Harvard Business School, to a commission whose purpose was to find a better way to run the Post Office, which was in more of a mess than usual. The group was composed of ten men, all from industry or some other special interest group with the exception of Baker and David Bell of the Ford Foundation, who constituted what is known in political circles as the "public" representatives, possessing some degree of independence. At one of the early meetings the members of the commission were much impressed by Dean Baker's suggestion that they might do worse than turn over the parcel post system to private corporations.

This was a novel idea. But then most people don't know, and certainly the President never bothered to inform them, that the Dean of the Harvard Business School is also the chairman of the Transportation Association of America, a trade group of common carriers, which includes among its objectives: "Reduce government competition with, and threats of socialization to, one or more segments of the transport industry." Baker also sits on the boards of directors of Lockheed, Socony Mobil, which operates a large fleet of tankers, and the First National Bank of Boston which leads in financing the trucking business. Baker later said he believed it was at least possible to interest private enterprise in the parcel post since

73

it was one part of the postal system left that offered the opportunity of making money.

Baker is what is known as an "action intellectual." In his *Life* articles on this subject, Theodore H. White says the professors are a new "priesthood," and goes on to describe the Biblical Spectacle: "In the past decade this brotherhood of scholars has become the most provocative and propelling influence on all American government and politics. Their ideas are the drive wheels of the Great Society; shaping our defenses, guiding our foreign policy, redesigning our cities, reorganizing our schools, deciding what our dollar is worth."

White is a great admirer of these people. As power brokers, the professors act with one hand in the university and the other in a big corporation; they move in and out, using their prestige as scholars to advance the interests of the company; or on the other hand, using their influence with the company to help the university get research funds. In this sense they make themselves indispensable political agents.

Moreover, the form of the university itself changes. While the general citizenry may well believe the university interests itself primarily in educating students, in reality, universities are aggressive in advancing themselves as institutions in society, and this has led many of them rather far afield. Who would have thought, for instance, that American universities could be a major factor in pressuring Congress to keep the prices of medicine high; that the patents to the high-priced drugs are held by such universities as Rutgers and the University of Wisconsin?

Most often the professors are simply lobbyists for corporations, advancing the interests of their clients at the rate of $400 a day for their help. They are seldom taken for such, moving as they do beneath the cloak of distinguished degrees and university titles. Where the newspapers would rarely make note of the remarks of a registered lobbyist in the Capitol, a learned economist from an Ivy League university may well get two paragraphs for his views, even though they are not his opinions at all but those set out for him by some public relations man.

The "priesthood" swarms through Washington. Dr. Raymond Saulnier, the Columbia economist, stumbles through a long piece of set testimony as to why ITT should be allowed to merge with ABC, while the Federal Communications Commission examiner droops half asleep in his chair and the attorneys sit out front biting their nails. John Tukey, the Princeton statistician, who is also associate executive director of the Bell Telephone Laboratories, is in another room at this commission, leading a line of distinguished university economists who have been paid by the telephone company to come by and tell the FCC why the telephone rates are too low. If this becomes too tedious, it is possible to drop in on Professor Tetsuya Fujita from the University of Chicago, who has been hired by the British Aircraft Corporation to explain how its plane blew up in the middle of a thunder storm. Fujita is an expert on thunderstorms, which he studies under a National Severe Storms grant.

The Grocery Manufacturers Association hires Jesse W. Markham, a Princeton economist, to direct a study that will prove to the Food Marketing Commission that food prices really are rather low, and likely to go even lower because of the brisk competition among the chain stores. Meanwhile the National Association of Food Chains gives Roger W. Gray of Stanford University's Food Institute $100,000 for similar studies, which it is hoped will head off the marketing commission. Gray doles out the money in lots of $5,000 to professors around the country, who write papers; he sponsors a contest for the American Farm Economic Association, giving prizes of $1,000 each for especially brilliant papers on food marketing. Oddly enough, two of the professors whose work Gray originally sponsored win prizes. All of this is sent along to the Food Marketing Commission as evidence of what the economists think. The Commission never did publish Markham's study, since it relied on figures that showed the industry spent most of its research money in developing dog food.

One of the more discreet and most powerful of these underground lobbyists is John T. Dunlop, the Harvard economics professor. He is commonly regarded as chief spokesman in Washington for the construction trades unions. Dunlop is credited with having devised the strategy which brought these warring unions together, and won them unprecedented wage increases. The construction trades unions are segregated, and Dunlop shrewdly helps them devise policies that are meant to ensure things stay that way.

For instance, Dunlop is a consultant to the President's Committee on Urban Housing. In that capacity, he mediated an agreement among the contractors, government departments and trades unions for employment of blacks in construction projects begun under the Model Cities Act. That act specifically calls for employing the residents of the affected area in reconstruction. One section requires "maximum opportunities for employing residents of the area in all phases of the program and enlarged opportunities for work and training." That means hiring blacks as construction workers.

The construction trades control all hiring. They are not willing to discuss bringing blacks into the big new construction projects. However, Dunlop in a memorandum of agreement developed a scheme whereby it was made to appear that the unions would tolerate some blacks in the insignificant rehabilitation work performed under the Model Cities scheme. Under Dunlop's proposal two new categories would be established, "trainee" and "advanced trainee." The memo never says whether the trainees would ever get into the union, the only way for them to get permanent jobs. The trainees could work on demolishing buildings and on construction of buildings up to *four stories* in height. In lieu of the usual union fringe benefits, the blacks would get some indeterminate amount as an "allowance." Herbert Hill, the national labor direc-

tor for the NAACP, discovered Dunlop's memo before
it had been adopted, and once it was in the newspapers,
the behind-the-scenes negotiations in Washington were
broken off in embarrassment. But at this writing there
was every expectation that they would be renewed, with
Dunlop and his gang devising some new way to keep out
the blacks.

A sure-fire way to plead a cause and impress legislators
is to send them an article from a learned journal, supposedly written by some dispassionate professor. Actually, of course, he was slipped some money under the
table to write the piece. Lawyers practicing in Washington have reduced law journals to the status of publicity
releases. In 1957 Wright Patman, the Texas congressman, reported to the House of Representatives on the use
of journals for public relations purposes.

"Other lawyers who have cases in court involving
problems arising under the Robinson-Patman Act are
busy writing law-review articles in which they are para-
phrasing and summarizing attacks upon the Robinson-
Patman Act in the Attorney General's report. In addition
to citing, as an authority, the report they helped write,
they also cite and rely upon writings of others who were
members of the Attorney General's committee. Some of
that self-lifting technique is utilized without informing the
readers that the authors of the writings are partisans ad-
vocating the same causes in pending court cases. Perhaps
this is not the rule-of-reason approach, but certainly it is
an approach in the direction of an effort of one to try his
lawsuit not in the newspapers but in law reviews.

"Recently there appeared in the *Yale Law Journal* an
article written by an attorney who was a member of the
Attorney General's committee. That article adroitly failed
to disclose that the author is affiliated with a law firm
presently opposing the government in a pending case arising under the Robinson-Patman Act. The article attempts
to deprecate the Robinson-Patman Act and proceeds to
argue many issues of fact and law arising under that act

and present in pending litigation. It is copious in its use
of footnotes citing 'authorities' upon which it relies for
support for the position presented. A substantial number
of all of the authorities thus cited, a total of fifty-seven,
were either to statements contained in the report of the
Attorney General's committee or to writings by members
of the Attorney General's committee. Actually the author
of the article appearing in the *Yale Law Journal* cited
seven times his own writings as authorities. If this matter
were not so serious as to its probable effect upon future
enforcement and interpretation of our antimonopoly laws,
this instance could be dismissed lightly as an amusing incident of one attempting to lift himself by his own bootstraps and the bootstraps of his colleagues."

Justice William O. Douglas has gone after the law reviews for failing to disclose what the authors are up to. In
a speech at Washington University in 1965 he listed off
various examples. "Another instance of non-disclosure involved a law review article on the concept of 'effective' or
'workable' competition," he said. "The article did disclose
that it was a revision of a report submitted by the author
to the Business Advisory Council. But it did not disclose
that the author had received more than $13,000 from the
council for this report and other work, nor did it disclose
that the council's special antitrust study fund (from which
this author was presumably paid) was obtained from con-
tributors of whom a majority were past or present de-
fendants in important antitrust suits."

Efforts to persuade law journals to insert disclosure
statements have been made by some universities. UCLA
is one—but opposed by others, including the Harvard
Law School.

The use of journalists as public relations agents, of
course, extends beyond the learned journals. I was
offered, but refused, $1,000 in Ford Foundation money
to write an article in the *New Republic* that was favorable
to New Careers for the Poor, a poverty program run by
an NYU professor.

The insurance business runs one of the cleverest public relations operations in the country. There are some 350 members of the American Risk and Insurance Association, Incorporated, a professional group of insurance and economics professors which maintains its headquarters at the State Farm Insurance building at Bloomington, Illinois. A questionnaire sent to the members of this association revealed that eighty of the 151 people who replied were either consultants or taught summer classes for insurance companies. Twenty professors said they were directors of insurance companies.

Each year the Institute of Life Insurance, the industry's public relations front, pays sixteen universities to run summer workshops in family finance. The program is put together by a national committee for education in family finance, which in the past was headed by Harold Hunt, a Harvard professor. The universities involved include, among others, Wisconsin, Oklahoma, Arkansas, UCLA and Penn State.

The idea is to bring high school teachers into the universities and teach them the importance of free enterprise so that they may in turn repeat the litany to their students. Along the way, there are plugs for life insurance. For example, in one class the teachers were asked to fill in a crossword puzzle. Number 22 across asked in eight letters to fill in the phrase, "Having insurance gives one a feeling of. . . . . . . ? The answer, of course, is S-E-C-U-R-I-T-Y. Or in nine letters, "What is a means of sharing risks?" I-N-S-U-R-A-N-C-E. People who are especially helpful to the insurance business get elected to the Insurance Hall of Fame at Ohio State University.

Over the years the drug companies have ingratiated themselves with the universities, especially the medical schools, by supporting research and handing out favors to the students. Pfizer and Merck provide scholarships; Roche Labs offers medical students a choice of one $20 textbook a year for each of four years. Lilly doles out stetho-

scopes; Lederle invites the medical student and his wife
along for a free weekend in New York City. After a tour
of the factory, the students are dined at places like Tav-
ern-on-the-Green. In the summer, pharmaceutical houses
hire medical students to sell pills door-to-door.

Moreover, it is not uncommon for companies to seek
out young clinicians to test new pills for them. The companies will offer a free batch of the new medicine, along
with three to five thousand dollars to defray administrative expense. One result is to get a young doctor involved
with the company so he will remember them in prescribing
drugs later on. But more important, the purpose is to get
rough, sloppy and inexpensive tests done so that the pills
can be slipped past the drug requirements of the Food
and Drug Administration. This is an old trick and has
produced unfortunate results. One of the investigators for
thalidomide was a doctor who gave pills to pregnant
women who had trouble sleeping. He kept a rough count
of how many women said they slept better after taking
the medicine, and would relay these counts to the company's research director. However, two of his patients
sued him for damages after taking thalidomide and giving
birth to deformed children.

Dr. Leo J. Cass, director of the Harvard Law School
Health Service, has tested numerous drugs for the companies. On looking into the Cass operation, the Food and
Drug Administration claimed some of the people he cited
in test statistics for one drug were dead. The FDA suspended Cass's license to investigate drugs. Cass claimed
there had been a mixup in the record keeping. Dr. Albert
Kligman of the University of Pennsylvania's Medical
School has directed research into 153 drugs for leading
pharmaceutical houses. The FDA said Kligman's research
on DMSO, a drug that was supposed to relieve arthritis,
was faulty. Whereas Kligman said twenty men received
the medicine twenty-six weeks, the FDA claimed some
got it for only sixteen weeks, and others quit taking the
drug before that. Kligman reported no severe reactions to

DMSO, but the FDA said it found that in at least one case there were severe reactions: a man's body broke out in a terrible case of hives. The testing of DMSO was halted because of eye damage observed in animals who had been given the drug.

Kligman's privileges as a drug investigator were withdrawn by the FDA for a time; they were eventually reinstated after the doctor gave the agency certain assurances concerning his test methods.

Dr. Chester S. Keefer of the Boston University School of Medicine is on the board of directors of Merck & Co., Incorporated. In August of 1962, during Senator Kefauver's fight to regulate the drug companies, Keefer appeared before the House Commerce Committee, and arguing the industry line, claimed that pharmaceutical firms use "extraordinary care in selecting highly trained clinical investigators." The chief investigator for an anticoagulant called Mer/29 was Dr. William Hollander, also of the Boston University School of Medicine. Hollander tested the drug for Richardson-Merrell. "I was amazed to learn that Dr. Hollander had very little concept of the tests he was attempting to interpret, and, indeed, did not have the slightest idea of the underlying physiological, biochemical and pathological basis for the determinations," says an inter-company memorandum from a medical specialist to an official. Another memo from R. H. McMaster, associate director of medical research to Howard W. Werner, vice-president for research, said: "Hollander mentioned the matter of his consultation fee. You will recall that we have had him on a personal retainer amounting to $2,400 per year in 2 semi-annual installments. If we wish to maintain this relationship . . . a payment of $1,200 is now due. My own feeling is that we can't afford to chance alienation of Hollander just now (perhaps I shouldn't regard this as blackmail)." Another memo suggests Hollander also wrote up publicity material on the drug. The communications cited above were introduced into a civil damage suit brought against Richardson-Merrell by people who suffered severe side-effects after taking Mer/29. Some of them lost their hair and developed cataracts in their eyes. One of these suits, brought in New York State, resulted in a $1 million judgment against the company. In Washington, D.C., a federal grand jury indicted the company for violation of the food and drug laws. On pleading nolo contendere, Richardson-Merrell paid a fine of $80,000.

Several universities have profited from royalties from patents they hold on medicines. Indiana University holds the patents to Crest toothpaste. Rutgers made several millions on royalties from patents to streptomycin. The Wisconsin Alumni Research Foundation at the University of Wisconsin provides the university with nearly $2 million a year, much of it derived from royalties from inventions that were made in the university's laboratories. Probably the most widely known of these is Warfarin, a leading rat poison, which can be combined with sodium and becomes useful in humans as an anticoagulant.

These relationships and others may serve to explain at least in part why American universities have lobbied the Congress on behalf of the drug companies against measures which would more clearly regulate the activities of that industry, and why they have been so adamant in opposing legislation which would work toward lowering the prices of prescription drugs. This is not the sort of thing one would expect of a university, but with the sole exception of Harvard, they are simply opposed to putting in the public domain the benefits of publicly sponsored health research, and through the American Council on Education, the presidents and prominent professors of various universities have worked to oppose changes in the patent laws that move in this direction. Indeed, the universities want to go in the opposite direction, and support legislation which would result in turning over to private interests the patents on all sorts of inventions resulting from public research, which, as a practical matter, means turning them over to large corporations to exploit on their own terms.

Over a number of years, there have been several attempts to change the restrictive drug-patent laws, which have coincided with a broad general debate within the government over what happens to inventions resulting from federal-financed research. Should they as a matter of principle be turned over to the inventor for his use or should they be placed in the public domain?

In medicine the seventeen-year patent works against competition, permitting the manufacturer to rig prices and control markets. An example may help to show what is involved here. Dr. Robert Guthrie, a Buffalo, New York, scientist, found an inexpensive way to tell whether or not a baby had PKU, which is a disorder tiny children get that leads to retardation. If it is discovered quickly, PKU can be prevented by putting the child on a special diet. Guthrie's work was supported by both the government and private foundations. In the interest of getting his invention on the market quickly so that as many people as possible could benefit from it, Guthrie did what the drug companies suggest is the American way. He took out a patent and licensed Ames Company, a subsidiary of Miles Laboratories, to manufacture the test kit. Guthrie himself refused royalties, turning what would have been his share over to a foundation. When the patent arrangements were completed, nobody thought to ask Miles what it proposed to charge. In his own laboratory Guthrie could produce a 500-test kit for $6, so he was rather stunned when Miles announced it would market the kit for $262. The company claimed the price was justified because of the high-quality sterile materials. But when it was asked whether its kit was superior in any way to the one made by Dr. Guthrie, Miles said there was no difference. Because of the high price, many public and private services which had wanted to use the Guthrie Kit could not afford to do so. Finally Guthrie got the patent annulled, and the test is now made cheaply and widely used. This is not an unusual example; indeed, there are thousands of pages of testimony taken by congressional committees, beginning with Senator Kefauver's own investigations in 1958, that show the very same pattern.

In a sporadic surge of populism Senator Russell Long tacked a rider on a health bill in 1965 that was meant to make sure this sort of situation could not happen with any invention in the field of health that resulted from publicly financed research. He proposed to place the patents to such inventions in the public domain. While the Senate had been arguing this business off and on for several years, the rider was a parliamentary trick by which Long aimed to circumvent a conservative subcommittee run by Senator John L. McClellan. McClellan was attempting to rewrite the patent laws from the other way around, and wanted a bill that would turn over all patents to the inventor of any inventions financed by the government.

Lister Hill managed the health bill on the floor, and he led the defense against Long. Hill's most useful tool in doing so was to read off one after another a hundred-odd telegrams and statements from university people opposing the Long rider. These had been obtained by the American Council on Education's lobbyist, Jack Morse. Some were couched in the usual academic goo: "This complex and important subject merits its own thoughtful and exhaustive study," said Robert F. Goheen, president of Princeton. Thomas H. Eliot, chancellor of Washington University, summed it up for the crowd when he declared, "Your existing patent laws on research and development have flourished and the nation benefited. Dealing specifically with universities, these are not profit institutions and any patent royalties are spent by them for the public benefit, for our universities must thrive if they are to provide good education for swiftly increasing numbers of Americans." This is a rather unpleasant way of saying the general citizenry should put up with a corrupt price system in order to support public education; pay higher prices for drugs so well-to-do children can go to Washington University.

University professors help the drug companies out in yet another way. They hire themselves out as expert witnesses who appear before Congress as part of a manufacturer's lobbying team. In 1961 Lloyd Cutler, the Washington attorney who, among other things, runs the lobby for the Pharmaceutical Manufacturers Association hired a group of distinguished professors to oppose the Kefauver amendments to the drug laws. Kefauver was trying to have the Food, Drug & Cosmetic Act changed so that the burden for proving a drug's safety and efficacy fell upon the manufacturer and not the government, as then was the case, and he also sought more effective regulation of the industry's pricing policies.

The drug companies employed Jesse Markham, the Princeton economist, and Bertrand D. Fox, director of research at the Harvard Business School, to work up a study of the industry. They in turn were able to call on the staff at Arthur D. Little & Company and a group of other consulting professors, who were hired to help stave off Kefauver.

The appearance of Markham and the Little people at these hearings was a humorous event, for everyone knew they were really public relations men disguised as professors. (A professor who testifies is always greeted grandly, the committee chairman often sarcastically addressing him as "Doctor" or "Professor," or should it be some high university official, "Dean," and the event begins with an absolutely endless recitation of the witnesses' degrees, clubs, books, associations and honors.) Markham began by promising to present "persuasive evidence that the ethical drug industry is more dynamic than most manufacturing industries and characterized by a relatively low and declining level of concentration." Yet when it came to illustrating what he meant by this, Markham pulled out a chart that showed companies which had 31.9 percent of the market in 1951 controlled 64.5 percent in 1960, thereby apparently making the opposite point. Both Markham and Richard Mannis, the representative from Little, insisted that price levels for prescription drugs had moved lower, not higher as Kefauver thought. Finally, however, when Mannis could not convince the senator of this, he admitted to never having studied price competition among the different drugs, and hence really didn't know much about it. Rather, Mannis said, he was thinking about another kind of competition, based on the "relative merits" of the different products.

For the main event of the day Cutler had dredged up Eugene Rostow, dean of the Yale Law School, Cutler's alma mater. Kefauver greeted this gentleman sarcastically, "You are listed in the press as testifying as Eugene V. Rostow," he said. "I take it that you are not speaking as dean or for the Yale Law School or for any institution."

"Oh, no," said Rostow. "I believe, though, Senator, whenever we appear, as one of my colleagues once remarked, it inevitably does involve the Yale name, and I am a firm believer in the principle of a very strict obligation on the part of any professor, whether he is a lawyer or an economist or a physical scientist, that when he appears on a public occasion of this kind to recall that his primary obligation is that of a professor always, not an advocate."

"Of course, I don't blame the PMA for trying to get somebody from Yale," Kefauver said. "It shows good judgment in that respect. But as I understand it, you are appearing here as an individual."

"Yes, sir."

"Having been employed by the PMA, or by the law firm representing them, to make a study and to make a presentation before this committee—is that correct?"

"That is right."

And so Rostow offered himself up with that charm with which one always recommends himself in academic circles: to be at once a professor but never an advocate, yet an advocate but never a professor. Rostow said he was not an expert on the drug industry; he was not an expert in patent law; and he was not an expert of the act whose amendment was under consideration. Having declared his basic ignorance of all matters at hand, he thereupon launched into a lengthy attack on the bill, quoting liberally from Jesse Markham's press releases, which the dean had been shown by way of background material.

Rostow is well known as the author of *A National Policy for the Oil Industry,* a work in which he argues for breaking up the oil industry because of its monopolistic tendencies. In the course of the book he suggests how the oil companies developed a monopoly by setting prices so as to result in excess profits of 14 percent after taxes. Yet in the drug industry where profits run to 20 percent after taxes he found the competition stimulating. If there were instances where it could be shown that the public suffered by a drug company's charging an unconscionably high price, then Rostow's solution was for the government to seize the patent, start up a factory on its own and manufacture and sell the product, thereby in all likelihood bringing upon itself a suit by the company involved for infringing the patent. But here is precisely the sort of idea corporations employ professors to propose. It looks both radical and novel, and since it is not taken seriously, therefore recommends itself as a subject for a research study.

This lobbying still drags on. Dr. Richard Burack of the Harvard Medical School published in 1967 a book called *Handbook of Prescription Drugs,* which lists the different prices for these medicines by their generic and not brand name, thereby helping the reader select the cheapest manufacturer of a drug. This was a daring move by Burack, one which should have been made by doctors years ago. Even the Congress, which refuses to regulate drug prices, could at least have gotten out a booklet of free information for the public. On the publication of Burack's book,

Senator Gaylord Nelson of Wisconsin revived the pricing issue and called hearings before a Senate Small Business Subcommittee. Once again the PMA dragged out Markham, the Little Company and a team of learned consulting professors from other universities, to whom they paid $40,000, to come and testify how well the drug companies competed with one another.

The PMA later gave the subcommittee a list of its fees. It paid $6450 to Paul H. Cootner of the Massachusetts Institute of Technology, $4500 to Markham, $4250 to Simon N. Whitney of New York University and $875 to John M. Firestone of City University of New York. Irving H. Plotkin, an MIT economist, got $10,250. Markham told Mark R. Arnold of the *National Observer,* "None of us made any pretense whatsoever that we were going down as completely objective professionals." And Cootner declared, "Nothing I said was either for or against the drug industry. All I said was there is a relationship between risk and return as a theoretical principle . . . That was deduced to be in support of the drug industry."

In the middle of the summer of 1967 the subcommittee received a long scholarly letter from a Dr. Alfred Gilman of the Albert Einstein College of Medicine at Yeshiva University in New York City. It began: "I wish to give you my views, as a pharmacologist, educator and co-editor of a well-known text, *The Pharmacological Basis of Therapeutics,* concerning matters related to prescription drugs that have been discussed before your distinguished subcommittee. I offer my comments in letter form, because my present schedule will not permit me an opportunity to appear in Washington. I trust, however, that this letter can be made part of the hearing record." Dr. Gilman went on to say that while generic drugs might appear to be the same as brand-name medicines, in reality they may well be made of inferior materials. The letter was signed "Alfred Gilman, Ph.D., William S. Lasdon Professor of Pharmacology and Chairman of the Department,

Associate Dean for Graduate Education." A copy was
sent to each member of the subcommittee. The staff was
intrigued by Dr. Gilman's remarks and asked him to testify, but he refused to do so. At last it became obvious
why Dr. Gilman didn't want to come. He told the subcommittee he was a consultant to three drug companies
and had been asked to write the letter by the president of
the Pharmaceutical Manufacturers Association.

When the government published its report during
1964, linking cigarette smoking with cancer and heart
disease, the professors and medical schools lost no time in
pitching in to help the tobacco companies ward off the
Public Health Service. This hasn't been much trouble
since the government does little to publicize the report.

University people helped the tobacco industry in several different ways. First, when it came to lobbying
against a proposed bill that would require the placing of
health warnings on each package of cigarettes, professors
came in before congressional committees, passed themselves off as expert witnesses and testified against the bill.
They never revealed that they had been hired by the tobacco companies. One of them was William J. E. Crissy,
professor of marketing and associate dean of the Graduate School of Business Administration at Michigan State
University. Crissy announced he was up on the latest in
student thought and psychological theory. He had observed that the modern student was rebellious in general,
and were the Congress to insist on placing a health warning in cigarette advertising, there would in all likelihood
be a terrible backlash, and to spite their elders, students
would smoke more cigarettes than ever before.

Sometime later Crissy admitted he was a consultant to
the tobacco industry. "They came to me for advice and
counsel," he explained. While his retainer did not require
that he himself testify, Crissy declared modestly, "Strate-
gically I was the best antidote to Paul Rand Dixon
[chairman of the Federal Trade Commission, who by
that time had already caved in to the industry]." Crissy

believed the advertising warning set a dangerous marketing precedent. What if automobile manufacturers were required to broadcast traffic deaths along with their commercials. "As I told my good friend Senator Neuberger," Crissy said, "contractors who build equipment for the Navy don't feel an obligation to talk about the death toll in Vietnam in their advertisements."

Several other professors also palmed themselves off as dispassionate witnesses. Darrell B. Lucas, chairman of marketing at New York University's Graduate School of Business Administration, said he received $3200 or $400 a day for "eight consulting days (or parts of days)." When Senator Daniel B. Brewster of Maryland made known his disgust at the lobbying activities, David R. Hardy, a lawyer who represents the tobacco companies, accused the senator of trying to smear the decent men who had been brave enough to testify. After all, Hardy said, everyone knew they were for the industry, even if nobody said it straight out. And by exposing them, Hardy thought Brewster's high-handed methods could "serve to close off scientific discussion on a matter of serious concern."

After the report came out, the tobacco industry placed a label on each package of cigarettes, warning of the possible dangers of smoking, in exchange for a government promise to keep its hands off cigarette advertising for four years.

While the industry was staving off the labeling law, it devised a system of financial grants to researchers in order to help persuade people that the cigarette companies are very much concerned about cancer and are working to produce a safer cigarette. More important from the industry's point of view, if the grants are spread around enough it may be possible to dampen whatever enthusiasm the recipients ever had for actively protesting the activities of the industry and coming out in the open against smoking.

The tobacco companies divide the research on health

between an organization called the Council for Tobacco
Research, U.S.A.—which was started in the 1950's, at
the suggestion of Hill & Knowlton, the public relations
company which advises the industry, as an effort to counter attacks then being made against smoking—and the
American Medical Association, in the hope that scientists
would become involved in problems of the tobacco industry.

Dr. Robert C. Hockett, the associate director of the
council, has been around since the early days and remembers that they had trouble with the original name, Tobacco Industry Research Committee, because the word
"industry" created a bad impression with the public. People sometimes think the council is just another front for
the tobacco industry, but they are wrong. While representatives of different industry organizations make up the
board of directors and provide about $1.5 million a year
in research funds, the actual affairs of the council are run
by a group of scientific advisors, most of them professors,
who dole out the research grants to themselves and their
associates.

Basically, the council tries to concentrate on what its
scientific advisors believe to be the real research problems, as unglamorous as they may seem to be. The council believes, for instance, that machines used to simulate a
person smoking are really not adequate and can provide a
distorted picture. Each person smokes a cigarette differ-
ently, Hockett says, and the council has been trying to
figure out a way they can produce an honest simulation.
The council also runs inhalation tests on white mice. (Dr.
Clarence Cook Little, the former president of the University of Michigan and scientific director of the council,
is an expert on pedigreed white mice, and this is a help.)
They have white mice smoking cigarettes five times a week
for two years, the average life span of the mice; and
Hockett says the mice seldom get cancer. These experiments
have led the council to the conclusion that smoking does
not cause cancer. "We feel people wouldn't get lung cancer

even if they were heavy smokers, if they were in good health," Hockett says. "We're trying to find out what contributes to the elements of susceptibility and resistance," he added, leading up to the main point of the council's work, which is to figure out, "What's different about people who get lung cancer from those that don't?" "The real key may be in the protection of the patient rather than in modification of tobacco," Hockett said.

The council's research is directed by a scientific advisory board which includes Dr. Kenneth Merrill Lynch, chancellor and professor of pathology at the Medical College of South Carolina; Howard B. Andervont, scientific editor of the National Cancer Institute; Dr. Richard J. Bing, chairman of the Department of Medicine at Wayne State University's College of Medicine; Dr. McKeen Cattell, professor emeritus of pharmacology at Cornell University's Medical College; Dr. Leon O. Jacobson, professor and chairman of the Department of Medicine at the University of Chicago and director of the Argonne Cancer Research Laboratory; Dr. Little; Dr. Stanley P. Reimann, director emeritus of the Institute for Cancer Research at Philadelphia; and William R. Rienhoff, Jr., professor emeritus of surgery at Johns Hopkins Medical School.

The members of this self-perpetuating body meet four times a year, and get $150 a meeting plus travel and incidental expenses. Almost all the members of the scientific board vote themselves grants, according to Hockett. There are seventy-five active projects.

Hockett and the others on the council fly around the country, trying to revive the spirits of the tobacco industry by highlighting the positive side of smoking. The *Tobacco Reporter* for May, 1967, said Hockett at the Tobacco Workers Conference in Williamsburg, Virginia, discussed the "physical benefits" to be had in smoking. There Dr. Hockett pointed out that nicotine was helpful in keeping people awake as well as soothing their nerves; that smoking aids the movement of the digestive tract and works as a laxative, and there is mounting evidence that continuous smoking can cure canker sores.

While the Council for Tobacco Research doesn't maintain much liaison with other major research bodies which are looking into the connection between cancer and cigarette smoking, it does keep in close touch with the American Medical Association's Education Foundation, which is carrying forward its own researches into this matter, with $10 million in funds provided it by the tobacco companies.

The AMA project began in 1964 at about the time President Johnson was trying to push Medicare through the House Ways and Means Committee. The AMA lobbyists were hard at work trying to hold the swing votes, one of which belonged to a Congressman John C. Watts from Kentucky, a big tobacco-producing state. Shortly before the Surgeon General announced his report, Dr. Edward Annis, then the president of the AMA, in an address before the Kentucky state legislature, said everyone knew about reports that smoking caused cancer, but doubted that they would stop people from smoking. What was needed was a massive research project to identify the causes of cancer and perhaps indicate some means for cure or prevention. "The AMA is not opposed to smoking," Annis declared. "It is opposed to disease." Shortly after this talk the cigarette companies gave the AMA $10 million for a research project on cancer and smoking. There was a widespread rumor at the time that in return for using swing votes to keep Medicare locked into committee, the AMA would willingly undertake a public relations gambit for the cigarette companies.

The AMA's researches into smoking and health are directed by Dr. Maurice Seevers of the University of Michigan's Medical School, a member of the Surgeon General's original panel. His group of researchers exchange information with the Tobacco Research Council and they coordinate their financing as well. When the grantee of one group runs out of money, the other picks him up. In addition, Dr. Bing of Wayne State sits on the boards of both groups, and Seevers tries to go to as many meetings of the Tobacco Council as he can.

I asked Seevers whether he expected the AMA researches to result in any significant findings, and he replied, "Hell, no." Seevers went on to point out that $10 million didn't amount to much when it came to cancer research, and indeed, its main value was in putting a little money into the hands of experts, who in exchange for receiving it, would introduce tobacco into their research. The AMA study is not primarily aimed at cancer, but concentrates rather on cardiovascular and respiratory diseases, and looks into the psychological problems caused by smoking.

Dr. Severs, incidentally, is a director of Miles Laboratories, the company which sold the $6 retardation test kit for $262.

In their desire for revenue, the NCAA in 1967, despite the opposition of the Ivy League colleges, voted overwhelmingly to accept cigarette advertising during the televising of college football games. The contract says that advertisers "shall not include drugs which are habit-forming, patent medicines, tonics of dubious purpose, laxatives, political organizations or organizations whose policies or purposes are controversial." Dartmouth believed that if laxatives were banned, surely tobacco ads also ought to be banned, since smoking was a danger to health. R. J. Reynolds, however, takes three minutes per game at $47,000 a minute.

Columbia University was in the midst of a $200 million fund-raising drive when it took on the new "revolutionary" cigarette filter invented by Robert L. Strickman, the small-town chemist, to make a fast dollar. The university hoped to accomplish this by playing on the public's fears of getting cancer from smoking.

According to one version of the story Columbia first learned about Strickman in 1967 through Robert Katz, a

lawyer who is secretary of Distillers Corporation. Katz
didn't have any ties to the university but he was grateful
to the doctors at the Columbia hospital for saving the life
of his son after a bad fall. Katz had heard about the filter
from William Suitt, a friend of his in the advertising business, who as Strickman's partner had been trying to figure
out a way to get the tobacco companies to use the filter.
Strickman previously had approached a number of companies, but they all gave him the cold shoulder. Katz's
idea of turning the filter over to Columbia had an obvious
advantage. The tobacco companies might not believe
Strickman but they would very likely listen to Columbia,
which from its position as an impartial institution of
higher learning would seem to be telling the truth. (In
fact, because of its greed, Columbia had its own reasons
for peddling the filter.)

Suitt is a clever fellow, and before long Strickman was
meeting with the Columbia hierarchy. The main negotia-
tor was William Bloor, the university's treasurer, a cold
and enigmatic man who dwells in Columbia's finance office just off Wall Street. The trustees established a special
ad hoc committee headed by Benjamin Buttenwieser, an
investments specialist and co-director of the $200 million
fund drive, to devise the contracts covering the filter. But
before accepting Strickman's gift, Columbia sent the filter
to Fitelson Laboratories to test its effectiveness, and retained David Thomas, vice-president of McCann Erick-
son International, to run taste tests. The toxicity tests
were made by Charles Umberger of the New York Medical Examiner's office.

It seems hard to believe that even at these early stages
Columbia didn't know what a controversial area it was
moving into. The cigarette companies were advertising
their new low-tar and nicotine-filtered cigarettes on television and in the magazines; and it was all over the papers
that new kinds of filtered cigarettes were less likely to
give one cancer. During the spring of 1967 the regulatory
agencies in the federal government were demanding that

networks make more time available for anti-smoking ads, and calling for curbs on advertising claims by the industry. The Department of Health, Education and Welfare was just finishing up another report that showed more conclusively than before that smoking caused cancer.

Despite all this going on, Columbia up to this time did not contact anybody at the Department of Health, Education and Welfare, a logical place, one might have thought, for the university to get some advice. The university did not even consult its own director of cancer research.

Moreover, some of the trustees had access to knowledge about the tobacco business and some interest in its future. Buttenwieser is a limited partner of Kuhn Loeb & Co., the Wall Street securities firm which on June 29, 1967, about two weeks before Columbia and Strickman publicly announced the filter deal, was selling $100 million of American Tobacco Company debentures. Harold A. Rousselot, associate clerk of the trustees, is a general partner in Francis I. Dupont & Company, also a leader in that syndication. Walter D. Fletcher, an emeritus trustee, is a partner at Davis, Polk, Wardwell, Sunderland & Kiendl, the New York law firm which represents Reynolds Tobacco Company. Maurice T. Moore, then the chairman of Columbia's board of trustees, is a senior partner at Cravath, Swain & Moore, another New York law firm which at the time of the filter discussions was representing P. Lorillard & Company, a tobacco company, in certain aspects of merger negotiations with Schenley Whisky. Grayson Kirk held 100 shares of tobacco stocks, which he sold shortly before the public announcement so as to avoid suspicion of conflict of interest. He also is a director of two mutual funds which have several million dollars in tobacco securities. While the news bureau of Columbia said the university owned no tobacco stocks, it did not reveal that the portfolio included $3 million in notes of Reynolds Tobacco Company.

I was curious to know whether these business contacts

influenced the university in any way in making its decision and I wondered also whether they raised any ethical questions for Moore and Buttenwieser, the two trustees most directly involved in deciding to take on the filter. When I asked Moore about this, he said the trustees took great pains to avoid anything that smacked of conflict of interest, and assured me there was absolutely no chance of any in this instance, and that everyone on the board had voted. I was especially interested in his law firm's relation to the Schenley-Lorillard merger proposal, since the price of Lorillard's stock rose on the basis of the filter announcement and in any case would be a factor in such negotiations. Moore said he personally had nothing to do with the Lorillard case, and that anyhow the firm's role involved a specialized side aspect. For his part, Buttenwieser declined to be quoted. However, it is known that one of the reasons he was chosen to head the special ad hoc committee was that he did not own any tobacco stocks. Moreover, it is argued that had Buttenwieser been required to take notice of the sale of tobacco company debentures by his firm while at the same time he was negotiating a filter deal that might influence their price, then it would be impossible for any businessman to be a university trustee and run his business at the same time. One of the Columbia trustees said that the reason Columbia had moved so blindly into the filter deal was that it could not consult any of its business contacts for fear word would leak out and a speculative rush would be on in Wall Street.

If this were in fact the case, then it is an excellent argument for not selecting university trustees because of their business affiliations.

Somebody passed the word around Wall Street that Columbia had a filter, and in late June and early July tobacco stocks were moving slowly ahead, possibly under the pressure of speculative buying.

At the same time the Columbia University trustees had been polled by mail and approved the filter deal. (Arthur

Ochs Sulzberger, president of *The New York Times* and a Columbia trustee, subsequently told Morton Mintz of the *Washington Post* that he voted against accepting the patent.) Over the weekend of July 8 Columbia's news bureau wrote the press releases that announced the "revolutionary" new filter.

Meanwhile, in Washington, HEW was preparing to release a report with new information which suggested smoking caused disease. But its issuance was put off because John Gardner, then the Secretary, was ill. The tobacco company lobbyists hung around the Capitol, waiting to see the report. Finally, on the morning of July 12, HEW sent advance copies to the Capitol and informed interested congressmen that the report would be released that afternoon. The Republican members of the Senate Commerce Committee leaked the HEW release to the tobacco lobbyists.

Later that morning Earle C. Clements, former Senate majority leader and chief tobacco lobbyist in Washington, phoned his friends and acquaintances to tell them the good news: Columbia had the patents to a revolutionary new cigarette filter that would make smoking safer. From this point on, Washington figured that the filter was an industry trick to draw attention away from the HEW report.

By early afternoon there was a significant rise in the price of tobacco stocks. At about 3 P.M., half an hour before the exchanges closed, Columbia's news bureau sent around word to the newspapers and wire services that there would be a press conference the next day "to announce a development of far-reaching importance which promises to benefit mankind by reducing the health hazards of smoking." When this news reached Wall Street, there was frenzied trading in tobacco shares. Reynolds headed the list at the New York Stock Exchange with a turnover of 218,000 shares; most issues closed the day $3 to $4 higher.

Columbia's announcement, of course, clarified nothing

but instead heightened anticipation and promoted speculation in the stock market. Its most immediate result was to blot out news of the government report on smoking. All of this worked in favor of the theory that Columbia was somehow tied up with the tobacco companies.

The next morning trading in tobacco shares got so hectic the New York Stock Exchange halted all transactions pending Columbia's press conference. It was at this affair that Grayson Kirk, then university president, H. Houston Merritt, dean of the Medical School, and Stickman met for the first time. Kirk, sounding as if he were the president of some cigarette company, declared, "Some time ago Columbia was offered an unusual opportunity to participate in an arrangement which our medical specialists here today believe may make a significant contribution to lessen the hazards of cigarette smoking . . . Columbia sat down several months ago to discuss with Mr. Robert Strickman his generous offer to turn over to the university the rights to his invention of a new type of cigarette filter—one that after a series of tests under the auspices of our College of Physicians and Surgeons showed a dramatic reduction in the inhaled tars and nicotine when compared with conventional filters. It has been demonstrated that Mr. Strickman's filter is approximately three times more effective in reducing tars and nicotine than the filters now used with the leading cigarettes.

"After extensive discussions with Mr. Strickman, the Columbia trustees voted to accept this transfer of the rights to the new filter. The formal agreement was signed last Friday. We are most grateful to Mr. Strickman for allowing the university to help in offering his great research advance to the world."

There was scant basis for this extraordinary claim. While Strickman said the filter would make smoking "materially safer," he would not say what the filter was made of. Strickman claimed he was only retaining a "small percentage" of the royalties for himself, but the details of the agreement between him and Columbia were kept secret. The test data were vague. Fitelson Laboratories had tested the Strickman filter for tar and nicotine, but as *Business Week* pointed out, the result of these tests showed that the filter on True cigarettes did better at removing tars and nicotine than Strickman's.

It is usual in these matters to run extensive tests on animals with a view toward possible side effects, but none had been made. And inexplicably, the physical description of the filter as presented by Columbia was not the same as that given by Strickman. According to Fitelson's figures different amounts of granules would have to be put in the filters for different cigarettes to achieve the same desired effects. Nobody really knew who Strickman was; he passed himself off as a "consulting chemist" who because his parents had died of cancer became determined to try to beat the disease, and had worked in a laboratory at home for the past seven years before "inventing" the filter—but Strickman had never written about cancer research in this area either for industry or for the government.

After Kirk made these further unusual claims, the stock markets once again opened, but this time the insiders were baling out of tobacco stocks. One of them was Floyd O. Shelton, who manages investments for the University of Texas. Shelton had been watching for a chance to get rid of the university's large tobacco holdings. Then he heard about the Columbia patent. "It sounded crackpot to me," he remembers, but then Shelton didn't care about that. He was grateful to Columbia for hiking the prices. That day Shelton dumped the University of Texas' holdings in Reynolds (about 59,000 shares) and American Tobacco (24,000 shares), picking up a profit of $350,000.

Not long after the press conference, Warren Magnuson, chairman of the Senate Commerce Committee, asked HEW to look into the filter claims. He then went ahead to schedule his own hearings.

Toward the end of the summer, shortly before Magnuson opened the hearings, members of the Commerce Committee staff met with three representatives from Columbia, including John Wheeler, its counsel, and told them that the committee's investigations had shown that the Strickman filter was of dubious value, producing results barely different from existing filters. This information was based largely on reports from tobacco manufacturers who had tested the filter. (By this time people in Washington had pretty much decided the industry was not tied up with Columbia in some ploy, but that something else was going on, and what it was, they couldn't figure out.) The Columbia representatives were told bluntly that Kirk could expect some hard questions when he appeared before the committee, and that he had better be ready with some straight answers. At this point two of the university representatives said they thought Kirk should come clean and admit that Columbia had made a mistake, that it didn't in fact know very much about the filter, and cut loose from the Strickman agreement. But Wheeler reportedly argued for a middle course: Kirk would humbly promise to conduct further, more detailed tests. This would give Columbia a hedge. If the filter turned out to be not much good or public pressure grew too strong, the university would back out a bit more tactfully and with less adverse publicity. On the other hand, if the filter worked and Congress got off Columbia's back, they could push on. Kirk adopted this line, and Congress let him alone.

In the fall of 1967 Columbia discovered additional information about Strickman. While Strickman made himself out to be a "consulting chemist," it turned out that he was a one-time vice-president and director of a company called Casavan Industries, Incorporated, which through various subsidiaries was in the business of making and selling construction materials. In 1963 a federal grand jury in Newark, New Jersey, indicted Paul R. Casavina, president and controlling stockholder of the firm, and certain other officers, charging them with stock fraud. The indictment charged that Casavan had defrauded investors by selling stock that was not registered, and by pyramiding the assets of the company in such a way as to give it the appearance of a growing and prosperous enterprise, which it was not.

Strickman himself was never named in any of the criminal actions. However, in two civil suits Casavan stockholders accused him of defrauding them, and asked for damages. One of the suits was settled out of court; at this writing the other is pending at federal district court in Newark. Strickman has not answered the suit.

The testimony at Casavina's trial suggests how the company had operated. Frank A. Cerruti, the accountant and himself twice convicted for forgery, described to a court a lavish brochure which Casavina had made up for advertising purposes. Entitled "This Is Casavan Industries, 1961," it purported to show marble from Casavan's Italian quarries being carried to the United States aboard Casavan's ships. Cerruti testified that he believed this gave a somewhat distorted picture, since Casavan owned neither ships nor quarries and was unable to purchase any marble because it had no money.

Cerruti remembered that the directors had approved Casavan's acquisition of Casavan Carrara Marble Company, which was also owned by Casavina and had a book value of $3,710. Casavan Industries evidently considered this an unusual investment opportunity, for the directors voted to pay Casavina 50,000 shares of stock worth $500,000 for his marble company. Strickman signed the deal for Casavan Industries.

Columbia's enthusiasm for Strickman as a business partner cooled not only because of this news, but because some scientists within the university had begun squabbling among themselves over the merits of the filter. A clique in the medical school held that the filter was everything it was claimed to be, and they infuriated the central administration by leaking complimentary stories to the newspapers. One appeared in the *Wall Street Journal* in mid-September and suggested that the filter tests Kirk had promised the Magnuson committee were nearly complete and that licensing agreements were about to be signed. Nothing happened, and *The New York Times* in mid-November reported an announcement by Columbia that tests on the filter were just then beginning. This was about the same time both Bloor and Kirk told me the tests had just been completed and were soon to be released. Dr. Ralph S. Halford, a chemist and special assistant to Kirk, was in charge of the testing, working with the U.S. Public Health Service, and by the middle of December had come to the same conclusion that the Senate Commerce Committee staff had reached four months earlier.

In December NBC attacked the Strickman filter as being no better than others on the market. Whereupon Strickman threatened to sue the network. The only useful information resulting from all this activity was Strickman's admission that his "small" percentage of royalties amounted to 15 percent for himself and 10 percent for his associates. By this time Columbia was earnestly trying to wriggle out of the deal. Psychologically, anyway, Strickman still held the upper hand. Columbia didn't want any more bum publicity in the midst of its fundraising drive, and it was frightened lest Strickman sue for breaking the agreement. To win a suit brought by Strickman against Columbia, the central university would need to turn on its own medical school—indeed, on the dean of the school—and admit that inadequate test data and poor judgment had caused Columbia to take on the filter in the first place.

One theory had it that the way to get away from Strickman was to take the filter and test it to death, two or three years if necessary, until people had forgotten the whole thing. But this seemed unnecessary when the chemist made an adroit move and set up a foundation, the proceeds of which would be given to Columbia's medical school. This arrangement was meant to work to Strickman's advantage, since he could continue to show some affiliation with the university. As a matter of fact, by that time it probably didn't make any difference whether he was connected with Columbia or not, since most people associated the filter with Columbia's announcement of a revolutionary break-through. Few papers had bothered to write about the filter after the initial announcement.

Nonetheless, the Senate Commerce Committee was insistent upon full disclosure of the matter by Columbia; and when the university tried to dodge around this, the committee's staff asked whether Columbia would care to undergo another round of public hearings. Rather than that, Columbia finally agreed to send detailed test results of the filter to the committee, which could then make them public, meanwhile handing back the patent rights to Strickman and announcing the university was not in a position to run the sort of business enterprise that was necessary to handle such an operation.

In July, Kirk had claimed that the Strickman filter had been demonstrated to be three times more effective than other filters on the market, but Dr. Halford's test data showed the filter was an average 15 percent more effective in removing tars and nicotine than cellulose acetate filters, which are not the most efficient filters on the market. Columbia refused to comment on these test findings. Whereas Kirk had said the new filter would lessen the hazards of cigarette smoking, and Strickman claimed it would make smoking "materially safer," at the news conference where he announced the break-away from Columbia, *The New York Times* reported: "Mr. Strickman and his associates reiterated assertions they had made from the beginning that no health claims were being made for the filter." Meanwhile Strickman announced he had signed licensing agreements with two Canadian companies, for $250,000 apiece.

Thus Strickman used Columbia to set himself up in business. Of course, he never could have succeeded without the greed of the university's managers and trustees. Looking back on the deal, Maurice Moore explained once more why the university took on the filter. "It looked like it might make money," he said.

Since 1958 the U.S. Public Health Service and the automobile manufacturers have financed research into the cause of automobile accidents by the Cornell Aeronautical Laboratory, a subsidiary of Cornell University. The laboratory sends investigators to the scene of an accident and they make a careful search for causes, including possible defects in the car's design. While Cornell has detailed statistics showing the defects in different makes of automobiles, it refuses to make this information public. Rather, the details are sent along to the auto companies on the theory that they know best how to make the necessary improvements, while the laboratory sends off bland general reports to the Public Health Service.

A study of car-door latches financed by both the Public Health Service and the Automobile Manufacturers Association and sent to the association for distribution to its members in November of 1964 shows how the industry used the results of the Cornell researches. The study showed that doors on General Motors autos were torn off much more often than those on cars made by other manufacturers. In his hearings held on auto safety, Senator Abraham Ribicoff introduced this study into the committee record, and Senator Robert Kennedy got into an argument with Harry Barr, GM's vice-president for engineering.

"Do I understand you that you haven't studied these records at all?" Kennedy asked Barr. "Was this information made available to you prior to the time that the chairman gave you the report of Cornell?"

"Senator Kennedy, I have not observed this personally," said Barr. "I am sure if the data is available we do have it in General Motors."

"Isn't it well known in your company that Cornell makes these studies?"

"Yes, sir."

"As everybody considers this an important matter, I would think that you would have a close working relationship with Cornell."

"We do have," said Barr.

"And with their studies?"

"We do have."

"How can you appear before this committee and not even know about it?" asked Kennedy.

"I believe the data requires more study on our part, sir," replied Barr. "We do have information here on the General Motors doorlocks, and we are very good in this area."

Actually, the central purpose of the Cornell researches was to provide a sort of intelligence network for the automobile industry, paid for in part by the general public and run by a leading university. Had Cornell really been devoted to independent scholarship, it would have made this controversial information public, and it might have steered people away from buying GM cars and saved their lives. Or as in another instance, the laboratory might have publicly revealed in 1961 or 1962 that the General Motors Corvair was of questionable design, consisting, as it did at that time, of a strange rear-axle arrangement where the wheels turned in, flipping the car over and a steering column which came down in front of the forward bumper, so that when the car collided head-on, the steering column acted like a skewer, ramming back and through the driver. And it was likely that were one to have a head-on collision in a Corvair, the gas tank would catch on fire since it was placed directly above the driver's knees. Thus, pinioned to the front seat by the steering column, the driver very probably would be burned alive. But Cornell never made this information public, and it never in any substantive way pushed the campaign against the auto industry for safety regulation. During one of these hearings into auto safety, Senator Vance Hartke struggled with Ira G. Ross, the laboratory's president, to try to find an answer as to why it would not let the information out, at least to the man involved in the accident under investigation.

"What about the person who is involved himself?" asked Hartke. "You are making a study of this kind. What good reason, psychologically, legally, or any other base you want to use, would you have for denying the information that you have received as a result of investigating his particular situation, for denying it to him?"

"That is a delicate question of ethics." Ross said, "I agree—"

"Why is it a delicate question of ethics? I don't think ethics is involved."

"You do," Ross said. "You were pointing up an ethical issue."

"No, I'm not asking ethics at all," said Hartke, growing short-tempered. "I am asking you why a man who is involved in an accident should be denied on any ground the material which you have been able to adduce through research on his particular case? Why isn't this his personal right, not a question of any ethics? Why is he not told as a matter of right?"

This argument went on for a while, and then Ross said, "Well, the issue here is very clear, and it has been our experience, and this is not conjecture, this research is experience with people who have done research and I have heard a little too much conjecture in the area, that we cannot, except as we make a precommitment to local authorities—"

"I didn't say anything about local authorities," replied Hartke. "I haven't mentioned local authorities. I mentioned one man."

"All right. You have implied precommitment to him, if you are doing this kind of research, but you will not disclose the data in court, because he doesn't know—"

"Wait a minute," said Hartke. "Just a minute. Nobody has mentioned court. Every time you come in with an extraneous factor. I want to know why can't you give it to him?"

"All right. That is a fair question."

"Sure it is," said Hartke, "I have asked it three times. It ought to be fair. Come on, let's get with it."

Ross then said, "I feel that if I give this man . . . the data you asked about, I will be blocked in my next investigation by the fact that I have done so, and I consider I have an obligation to the public at large which is fully as great as my obligation to that man."

While Ross said he refuses to tell the individuals actually involved in accidents what its researches discovered, the laboratory seems to have been more than willing to dig up details of individual cases to help manufacturers out of embarrassing situations. In the book entitled *The Rational Manager,* by Charles H. Kepner and Benjamin B. Tregoe, the authors describe how the automobile companies sought to ward off lobbyists from a safety-glass manufacturer who was trying to convince a state legislature that safety glass used by the auto makers was dangerous, and that, rather, they should be made to buy glass made by the company that had hired the lobbyists. To make the point, the lobbyists sent around a picture of two young girls allegedly scarred by flying glass of the sort then used by Detroit. The auto companies worked fast to track down the two girls and find out every detail about the case. They called insurance company officials, lawyers, police, and on receiving a tip from a local police officer that the case had been reported in detail to the Cornell Aeronautical Laboratory, the auto company people followed this up, providing themselves with exact details of the crash so they could best knock off the lobbyists. The Cornell crowd, incidentally, denies any knowledge of this incident.

Even though Cornell got keel-hauled before the Congress and shown up as an industry front, they haven't changed policy. More federal money than ever goes to the laboratory for research into auto accidents, and it still sends the details to the auto manufacturers, but gives the public only generalized statements. At this writing, the laboratory is undertaking a research study on Volkswagens for that company. This entails a search of the lab's crash records, which were collected in part with public funds, but the results will be sent to Volkswagen and not generally given out.

I asked James Perkins, president of Cornell University and then chairman of the laboratory's board of directors, why it did not reveal the automobile data publicly. He said that should the lab reveal its findings, then in all likelihood the companies would withdraw their support; and he went on to point out that from Cornell's view, the laboratory provided a neat solution all the way around, for while it was connected with the university, it was, in fact, separate from it, and therefore able to take on these industrial research missions, which would be hard to get away with on the campus itself where the academics might insist on timely publication of the results.

And this business still goes on. In 1967 interest was revived within the government for seeking alternate propulsion systems for automobiles because of air pollution and congestion in cities. This led to speculation about the feasibility of an electric car, an idea which the auto companies have always passed off as costing too much and, in general, as impossible to make. They have also maintained that autos don't contribute significantly to air pollution. The Commerce Department established a special committee to look into air pollution and the alternatives to internal combustion engines. One of the members of this group was Dr. Manfred Altman, who directs the Institute for Energy Conversion at the University of Pennsylvania. In 1966 Dr. Altman had expressed a good deal of interest in the electric car, and at that time had announced he was a consultant to General Motors on the subject. In the spring of 1967 Dr. Altman's institute got a $300,000 contract from the Department of Housing and Urban Development, which also was intrigued by electric cars, to look into mini-cars that could run in cities. Altman promptly turned around and subcontracted the engine and car-design part of the study to GM, because as he later declared, "GM knows how to build vehicles." Altman said that while he was no longer a consultant at General Motors, it was he who had interested the company in the whole business of mini-cars to begin with. So the government hired the leading auto manufacturer which had fought new car motors and designs to make one for it. GM proposed an eight-foot vehicle powered for the most part on a motor scooter engine, with a lead acid battery to help out in tight spots, which would cost as much as a Volkswagen.

So the professors mess about in politics. "The new action-intellectuals have transformed the ivory tower," says Theodore White, who loves the professors. "For them it is a forward observation post on the urgent front of the future—and they feel it is their duty to call down the heavy artillery of government, now, on the targets they alone can see moving in the distance. Courted by politicians and press, suspected alike by men-of-affairs and ivory-tower colleagues, the action-intellectuals worry about the contradictory tugs of pure contemplation and contaminating involvement. Yet they cannot draw back."

6. War

Because of growing student and faculty protests during the fall and winter of 1967, the faculties and administrators of many of the larger universities disavowed affiliation with secret research projects. The federal contracts manager at the University of Michigan said, "There is no classified research on this campus." Yet at the same time the university's Willow Run laboratory was working on a classified counterinsurgency project in Thailand. Grayson Kirk, then head of Columbia, said he was against classified research, and then described the secret antisubmarine warfare research performed in the university's Hudson Labs. The Students for a Democratic Society (SDS) revealed that a research project in the School of International Affairs had been financed by the CIA. Asked how this happened, Maurice Moore, chairman of the university's trustees, said, "I can't remember. How would you know what the CIA was 'funding'?"

Dr. Robert Goheen, president of Princeton University, also stated that he was against secret research, and yet just down the street on the campus, guards patrolled in front of a secret government-financed code-breaking center. A Stanford University press release suggested that the university was tightening its rules on classified research, when, in fact, it had merely rewritten the rules so that the university's educational philosophy could now easily embrace $4 million of secret research in its electronic laboratory.

In the spring of 1967 the House Appropriations Committee asked John S. Foster, Jr., director of research and engineering for the Pentagon, whether the universities had tired of their national responsibility and were leaving the Defense business. Foster said that as far as he knew only Harvard had a policy against classified work, although there was some talk that the University of Pennsylvania was reducing its involvement because of student protests against a government gas contract. (As a matter of fact, while Harvard has a policy against secret research, its professors are among the most valued military advisors in Washington. As for Penn, it has joined with other universities around Philadelphia and established a center where its faculty can continue secret research.) A year later Foster was back before the Appropriations Committee. He said that the contributions of the universities were more important than ever, and he had put through a new scheme called Project Themis to bring in some of the smaller colleges which heretofore had been excluded from Defense work. The schools were eager for the business and the Defense Department received research proposals from 173 of them, 42 of which obtained funds. So, if anything, there were more universities involved in Defense research in 1968 than before.

The universities' war machinery is arranged in a hierarchy. At the top is the University of California's Radiation Laboratory, which through its branch offices at Livermore and Los Alamos designs and builds prototypes of H bombs. The scientists who work at the Berkeley end of the lab say they have nothing to do with the dirty stuff at the other labs, but according to one young postgraduate physicist who wanted to work at the Radiation Laboratory, Dr. Edward Teller pointed out to him that while he could work in Berkeley, the only real way to make advancement at the lab was by getting into the secret work at Livermore and Los Alamos. In truth, the director of the lab sits at Berkeley and sets priorities for all projects and argues for them with the government.

The University of California, as befits the main university munitions dump, has what is in effect an interlocking directorate with the Pentagon. Dr. Charles Hitch, the president, was McNamara's assistant, and three consecutive directors of Defense Research and Engineering have come out of the Radiation Laboratory.

The hierarchy reflects a broad variety of interests. MIT and Johns Hopkins run centers which design missiles; half of MIT's budget and three quarters of Johns Hopkins' budget come from running defense labs. Cornell designs more effective bombs for Vietnam; Princeton breaks codes and runs conventions for the CIA. Michigan is first in photo reconnaissance and helps out with counterinsurgency. Pennsylvania and fifty other universities have recently been involved in chemical, germ and biological warfare research. According to John Foster, Princeton and the Davis campus of the University of California are working on new ways to get leaves to fall off trees, thus helping us to defoliate more of Vietnam. The University of Pittsburgh's Washington office is noted for its new tank gun sights and clever methods of sowing river and beach mines. The state college system of California runs a leadership project to teach young Vietnamese to think like Americans. And the University of Rochester in upstate New York manages the Secret Center for Naval Analysis in Alexandria, Virginia.

The most interesting of these military installations are those that are run by professors concerned with what they consider to be an implementation of a design for small tactical war. These are the liberal ideologists, or perhaps more accurately, the liberal propagandists. Through its Aeronautical Laboratory, Cornell University has lent its name to this business, and among similar intellectual enterprises it is highly regarded.

At the end of the second world war Curtiss-Wright was going out of the airplane business, and rather than sell its laboratory at Buffalo, New York, to a competitor, sought to place it in more or less neutral hands by giving it to a university. The laboratory, worth $4.5 million, was first offered to the University of Buffalo, which turned it down, then to Cornell, which after an initial hesitation finally agreed to take it on.

At this time university engineers were anxious to pursue large-scale experiments, and one way to pay for this was to run a research and development laboratory which would cater to industrial clients, thereby raising the money to pay for the equipment. (This, of course, turned out to be wrong, since the government financed all the research.) Anyway, in 1946 the university took over the lab, holding all the stock, and named it the Cornell Aeronautical Laboratory (CAL). The laboratory gives Cornell $50,000 a year for scholarships in engineering, and every so often a professor from the university will fly up to Buffalo twice a week and teach a course. A few graduate students work on theses at the lab, and it is not uncommon for Cornell engineering students to get some practical experience there during the summer; but that's about all the university gets out of the deal.

In the lab's 1965 annual report—beneath impressive photographs of James Perkins, president of Cornell and chairman of the laboratory's board of directors, and Ira G. Ross, president of the laboratory—there is printed this introductory message: "The modern American university is concerned with the discovery, transmission and application of knowledge. While mutually complementary, these three functions require innovation in organization and structure to bring them into effective relationship. Specifically, the predominance given applied physical research during the national emergency two decades ago raised a postwar challenge to continue the response to needs of civilian and military technology while avoiding distortions of teaching and the quest for basic discovery.

"Cornell Aeronautical Laboratory is one of the many experiments toward this end. As a separate entity from the teaching campus, its mission is to explore developing technology for ideas of potential utility, to shape and evaluate them through feasibility experiments and to advance them toward useful application."

CAL, free to develop its own staff and direction under the shelter of Cornell's name, performs more than 90 percent of its work for the government, and three quarters of this is for the Defense Department. Since 1946 it has handled $250 million in research contracts, and has revenues of about $26 million a year. Sixteen hundred people work there, most of them in the lab's headquarters, a long three-story building near the Buffalo airport; forty others work in an operations office in Washington. The lab maintains a testing ground for ammunition in upstate New York along with a special radar installation there. It maintains a fleet of three airplanes for special testing. In recent years it has diversified, with emphasis on research into automobile accidents.

CAL has a number of specialties. It helped Johns Hopkins University with the design of an early Bumblebee missile for the Navy, then went on to do the design work for the Army's Lacrosse missile. It works on a continuing program for the Air Force—a specialty being the study of how long-range ballistic missiles can be slipped through enemy defenses by masking the warheads as they come down or by sending along decoys to draw the enemy fire, thus permitting the real warhead to zing in on the target. At the same time it designs ways of distinguishing incoming enemy missiles—how to sort out the real warheads from the decoys and knock out the real ones.

But probably CAL is best known because of work done for the tactical air force, which directs the strike aircraft used in Vietnam, but which never received much attention during the days of General Curtis LeMay, who was especially enthusiastic for global war with SAC bombers flying constantly around in the air. But with the advent of the Kennedy Administration, and its interest in small wars and counterinsurgency, the tactical air force and

CAL played a more important role. As Perkins put it, CAL had a reputation for knowing "how to fight small wars."

Under the secret PENVAL project, CAL, using its own three planes, has developed techniques by which the U.S. attack aircraft can sweep in low over the ground and dart under radar nets to drop their bombs on North Vietnam. CAL's other specialty is photo reconnaissance in places like Vietnam and Laos. Since these unarmed planes have to fly into enemy territory, CAL works on ways of designing aircraft so they won't show up on radar screens. It also has an elaborate camera division, which not only does the standard work with infrared imagery, but in addition has developed "spatial filtering," which helps show up objects on the ground. Not long ago the laboratory designed a multi-camera aerial photographic system which makes it possible for a plane to come in over the Vietnam jungle and take the same picture at the same moment with different kinds of cameras and on different kinds of film. These different pictures can then be stored in a computer, which on request will produce them on a screen. It has been suggested that CAL did some of the work on the U2 reconnaissance efforts, but Ross denies this. He said the laboratory had worked from time to time for intelligence agencies, but wouldn't say which ones. The laboratory also periodically sends consultants to advise the military in Southeast Asia.

CAL has a number of other interesting projects. It helps the Army design traffic-control systems to keep its planes from colliding with one another over the battlefield. It works on antisubmarine warfare for the Navy; and CAL always has had expertise in bombs. As bombers started flying faster and faster, CAL created new devices to adjust the speed and trajectory of the falling bombs. In Vietnam some of the explosive effect of bombs is absorbed in blasting away the heavy vegetation, thereby reducing the range of impact. CAL is working to solve this problem. In addition, the lab worked on gadgets which

track mortars back to their sources and designed a new
family of weapons, projected for the 1980's, involving the
use of high-speed projectiles and laser beams. It also
made something called a "Man Amplifier." This device
strapped on a combat soldier makes him into a superman,
allowing him to pick up objects many times his own
weight.

Ross once said the laboratory's first goal was to innovate for "public service." Perhaps this refers to CAL's development of gas for war and control of domestic rioting.
The laboratory has developed three new kinds of weapons for disseminating this gas, and while this work is secret, Perkins admits it concerns aerosol sprays. He insists
that CAL doesn't actually make the gas itself; it only
helps the Army Chemical Corps find the most effective
way of using the nonlethal gas.

Apparently most people at Cornell University were
fairly well pleased with the laboratory, or at least what
they knew of its work, until recently. It was referred to
on the campus as the "stepchild," and whenever the subject came up, Perkins or Ross would speak about technological innovation, public utility and service. However, in
the summer of 1967, CAL made the mistake in its house
organ of boasting about being hired by the Defense Department's Advanced Research Projects Agency to run
part of a counterinsurgency project in Thailand. CAL
would help fend off "foreign-led infiltration and subver-
sion" in Thailand by building a rural security system.
This announcement infuriated a group of Cornell history
and social science professors who were gathering material
in Southeast Asia; they felt that if the university and laboratory were regarded by their contacts as one and the
same, they might be considered spies and their contacts
lost. They mounted a campaign within the administration,
and by February of 1968 the trustees of the university
had voted in principle to separate Cornell from the laboratory. What this in fact means is unclear at this writing
since the university holds all the stock to the laboratory

and it has a book value of $14 million. The lab would find it extremely difficult to buy the stock back at this price. And instead it hopes the university will settle for $5 million, which represents the worth of the plant itself; a deal could be worked out where CAL leases the plant from the university over a period of years.

The more fundamental issue of Cornell University's asserting control over this laboratory's technical operations was not seriously raised; nor was there any real argument among the faculty over the political significance of its work. Instead the matter was resolved on the narrow basis of how best to accommodate two groups of warring scholars without harming Cornell University's image in the process.

The University of Michigan's Willow Run Laboratory also works on photo-reconnaissance measures for the military, and along with CAL, is involved in counterinsurgency in Thailand. Willow Run has an annual budget of about $11 million, most of it from the Defense Department, and for some time has been recognized as an expert in infrared imagery. About 160 undergraduate and graduate students have secret clearances for their work at the labs. Willow Run, like Cornell, maintains its own fleet of airplanes.

Because of its intimate ties with the military over the years, it seemed natural enough for Willow Run to accept the Pentagon's invitation to send out some men to Thailand and set up a laboratory to train the Thais in photo-reconnaissance methods. This was part of an extensive U.S. effort to spot communist movements in the northeast of Thailand. The University of Michigan's part in the Thailand project remained secret until the fall of 1967, when the *Michigan Daily* made it known. The university then declared the project was nearly finished; however, Willow Run had consultants in Thailand in the winter of that year.

Dr. James T. Wilson, who directs the university's Institute of Science and Technology, which oversees the activities at Willow Run, said that in 1964, when they took up the Thailand work, there had been hope for containment in Asia and they had gone in with that end in mind. Dr. Harlan Hatcher, then the president of the university, put it more simply: he felt the Willow Run projects were a service to the nation. After all, he said of the reconnaissance missions, "You find yourself in Vietnam. American boys are being waylaid and destroyed."

Among the most active propagandists for our line in Southeast Asia is the Stanford Research Institute, the subsidiary of Stanford University, which is involved in war research. It was at SRI in the early 1960's that Professor Eugene Staley came up with the idea of manipulating the South Vietnamese population in our interests by setting up the futile strategic hamlet programs. More recently William Bredo, an SRI researcher, set off on a more enterprising project for AID—this one to find out just how many of the Vietnamese really wanted land reform. Bredo said it was surprising but that nobody really knew who owned the land in South Vietnam, nor how the South Vietnamese felt about land reform. He got together a team of experts, none of them able to speak Vietnamese. The plan was to get by the language barrier by subcontracting with a Vietnamese research firm to distribute questionnaires among the populace while the SRI team, some of whom could speak French, would discuss the situation with the village elites. This study, which could go on for months, was turned down by a number of other universities, who thought it was an obvious stunt by AID to prevent land reform.

According to Weldon B. Gibson, president of the institute, SRI doesn't want to get involved in ideological questions in determining whether or not to perform research; SRI is only concerned with whether the work offers a stimulating technical question. For instance, SRI does not want to be associated with research on gambling and vice, which wouldn't help the institute's image with the public.

Gibson asked himself rhetorically, "Would we develop a more destructive atomic weapon? Yes, if there were a need for it and the contract was there. We don't have any crusades," he added.

Counterinsurgency, or the manipulation of the internal politics of foreign countries, is very much a part of limited war, and is the source of another major liaison between universities and government. "I used to think the CIA was some horrible fascist conspiracy," remembered a student leader of the 1950's. "Then I discovered it was a little treasure trove of liberalism, the one refuge for liberals during the McCarthy period."

"Why did so many turn so willingly to the CIA for help?" Andrew Kopkind asked in the *New Republic*. "Because, in the first place, it had the money. Also it was audacious; it was concerned about foreign governments-to-be; it appreciated that anti-communism is not salable in most countries unless it is wrapped in a progressive package. CIA needed the American left, and the American left was flattered to be needed. Each served its own needs in serving the other's. Labor officials, intellectuals, churchmen and the like found money and support for their pet projects at the CIA when they had been denied by more cautious private foundations. A case in point is the Independent Research Service, a student organization founded in the months between the Vienna Youth Festival of 1959. American students wanted to attend the festival, but not on the 'official' delegation, considered to be pro-communist. Attempts were made to get private support for an anti-communist delegation, but foundations shied from any contact with the festival. Enter the CIA which underwrote the Independent Research trip and began a long close relationship with the organization and its directors. This experience was repeated hundreds of times during the height of the cold war in the late forties and fifties."

Ramparts magazine and many newspapers documented case after case of the CIA's interest in student groups.

But what is interesting is the process by which the students were brought along. After leaving college a promising student leader might be invited to attend the National Student Association's summer International Student Relations Seminar (ISRS), where he could meet former NSA officials and discuss international student politics. Among the NSA people were CIA agents. Participants in the seminar boned up on a book that recited NSA's history, and in particular its relations with the communist International Union of Students. The book was published by the University of Pennsylvania's Foreign Policy Research Institute, a recipient of CIA funds. After the seminar the student leaders were sent to an NSA congress. There NSA's "old boys" kept an eye out for men they wanted to run the association. Some were students who had already been exposed to previous seminars. If they did not become officers, students who attended the seminars could go to work for NSA either at its Washington headquarters or abroad as overseas representatives. The CIA would attempt to recruit the most promising types, who preserving their cover as student leaders could then work their way into one or another of the agency-supported foundations or student groups.

The CIA's old-boys network was extensive. After graduating from the University of Michigan in 1954, Harry Lunn became president of NSA, then turned up in the Air Force in both Washington and Paris. He later became executive director of the Foundation for Youth and Student Affairs (FYSA) in New York. Over the years FYSA has supplied up to 80 percent of NSA's international budget. Lunn would always appear at the summer seminars to brief student leaders and meddle in NSA elections. In addition to running FYSA, Lunn acted as a broker for the other CIA fronts. When NSA moved from Philadelphia to Washington in 1965, it had some difficulty finding a building. The officers were put onto another old boy: Leonard Bebchick, an international affairs vice-president of NSA in 1953 and now a Washington lawyer who practices before the Civil Aeronautics Board and represents the local Democratic Party in Washington. Bebchick arranged for the association to take over a large building in Washington on a free fifteen-year-lease. The Independence Foundation, a channel for CIA funds, paid the mortgage.

Students attending the NSA's International Student Relations Seminar two years ago remember going to a cocktail party in Washington at the new P Street offices of the Intercontinental Research Company, Incorporated, which as luck would have it had an office over the Women's Strike for Peace. IRC, Incorporated (never incorporated in the District of Columbia), was said to have been set up for former NSA officials who had won an unusual open-ended contract to "advise and consult" with the Agency for International Development on educational matters. One of the founders of IRC, Incorporated, was Robert Kiley, a 1958 graduate of Notre Dame and 1958-1959 president of NSA. From 1962 to 1964 he was vice-president of the World Assembly of Youth, another recipient of FYSA grants. Kiley lived in a rather grand house in Georgetown with Anthony Smith, a Williams graduate who represented the NSA in Paris in the early 1960's. Smith also worked at IRC, Incorporated. Both men, in fact, worked for the CIA. Kiley was head of the covert division which handled student affairs, and had represented the agency on the U.S. government's interagency youth board.

Two brothers, Manuel and Bob Aragon, helped set up IRC, Incorporated. Manuel was NSA's Latin American representative between 1958 and 1961, and served as the association's delegate to various international student meetings in Peru, Switzerland and Canada. In addition to his activities at IRC, Manuel was vice-president of the International Development Foundation, a CIA-funded operation which among other things sought to organize peasants in Latin America. Late in 1965 Manuel supposedly left his post at IDF to work in the regional-development administration of the Commerce Department. But there is no record of his employment there. Bob Aragon went to Latin America several times for the association. He was the Latin American representative for FYSA and maintained an office in Santiago, Chile, where he dealt with ORMEU, a Christian Democratic student-training project which had been identified as the recipient of CIA funds through FYSA.

The whole NSA structure was rigged. The old boys would manipulate elections and pick the top men. If necessary the candidates were given credentials to show they were enrolled in American universities. Eugene Groves, the NSA president who broke the ties with the agency, was a Rhodes Scholar in England when he was asked to run. NSA friends fixed him up with a graduate-school acceptance at Roosevelt University in Chicago.

In addition to constructing and manipulating this student propaganda arm, which must have been more trouble than it was worth to the CIA, the agency through foundation fronts dispensed funds to universities for work which interested it. MIT's Center for International Studies began as a CIA front. Michigan State's police-training program in South Vietnam was a dodge for the CIA agents. Cornell's School of Industrial and Labor Relations was supported by the CIA. And the agency ran a training scheme for Tibetans in Ithaca off the Cornell campus. Harvard University received money from more than a dozen CIA passes, and through its Marketing Institute, another CIA front, brought in Vietnamese to tell them about American industry. Among the things they got to see was the inside of an electric power plant in Cambridge. Columbia University's research on income in East Central Europe was financed by the CIA. The Dulles brothers graduated from Princeton along with a whole string of odd OSS men. These ties make Princeton University a handy place for the CIA to hold conventions from time to time. Joseph Strayer, a medieval historian, is perhaps the agency's most devoted consultant.

The Ivy League schools always have been a source of CIA employees. For instance, the dean of students at Princeton, William D'O Lippincott, and the former treasurer of Yale, Reuben A. Holden, were recruiters. At Princeton likely-looking candidates would get a card from the dean in the mail asking them to come along to Nassau Hall, the administration building, on a certain afternoon to discuss a confidential matter. A man would appear, shake hands, announce he worked for the government and hold out a form to be signed. On it was printed a statement in which the student promised not to divulge what would take place in the room. Once the form was signed, the CIA man identified himself. Having previously looked over the boy's university records, he then asked a series of questions. Satisfying himself with this material, the interviewer inquired whether the student would care to come by a certain classroom one Saturday morning and take the qualifying examination. At the appointed time a woman appeared and silently began passing out multiple-choice tests to a throng of prominent football players, socialites and assorted campus leaders who had stopped by. When the time was up, she collected the papers and disappeared. The boys were notified in the mail later on whether or not they were accepted.

In working through the CIA to secure money for research, or to get jobs, or in the construction of organizations which were made to appear open when they really were not, the intellectuals merely demonstrated they did not believe in open, democratic forms of government. And, indeed, they went further than this, for the operative theory which governed the liberals in the intelligence apparatus was, after all, that foreign policy *should* be determined and carried out in secret. The design was to be implemented by manipulation, and that manipulation, if worse came to worse, could be achieved by the methods of the police state. And it would be wrong to believe that the CIA conned the intellectuals, for in numerous other ways the universities and professors in them carried out schemes aimed at overthrowing or controlling foreign governments through violence and deception.

For instance, as part of the military's desire to keep underdeveloped countries away from the communists, the Defense Department brought up social scientists and put them to work playing around with psychological warfare. George Washington and American Universities in Washington, D.C., run two of the Army's centers which deal in different aspects of psychological warfare. George Washington's Human Resources Research Office (HumRRO) is concerned with teaching combat soldiers how to kill more efficiently, while American University's Center for Research in Social Systems (CRESS) collects intelligence on the countries of the third world and tries to build systems which will manipulate their policies so that communists can be kept out of power. Each of these different institutes is budgeted at about $3 million annually, with the respective universities drawing a fee of about a quarter of a million for administering their affairs; this involves managing a far-flung network of divisional posts in this country as well as offices abroad.

"HumRRO's mission is to discover, develop and apply human factors and social science principles and techniques to improve Army training and operational performance," says a blurb for the office. The research includes studies on the effect of music on the communists, a booklet on shooting entitled "How Fast Can You Hit Him?" and a work on urinary responses to stress. HumRRO employs about 300 people, who are spread around the country in seven different operations offices. Each office does something different. At Fort Knox it is armor; Monterey, recruit training; Fort Benning, infantry; Fort Bliss, air defense; Fort Rucker, aviation; Alexandria, language and area training. HumRRO people are on the go—whether it is working up a study to measure and manipulate visual hallucinations, going on patrols in Vietnam to get a feel for combat stress, or figuring out ways to get more firepower out of the famous gun ships which are used extensively in Vietnam. HumRRO has developed a short automated course in Vietnamese called MALT, works on counterinsurgency, provides hints for Army missions setting out from the Canal Zone to proselytize among the Latins. It published a booklet called "Optimum Kill Power of Man."

HumRRO employees are regarded not as full members of the George Washington University faculty but as "Adjunct Research Appointments." Dr. Lloyd Elliott, the university president, said some professors do their research at the office; there are a few joint projects among the office staff and university faculty, and he looked forward to more of this kind of interaction; half a dozen or so students carry out research toward master's and doctoral theses at HumRRO. Elliott was particularly enthusiastic about the training techniques involving computers, and believed that some of these might be put to practical use in slum schools. (Transferring military methods to slums is very big with the Defense Department and is part of Peacefare.) Elliott said scholars the world over were impressed by motivational studies at HumRRO, and one of the HumRRO people was off to Paris to deliver a lecture on the subject. Some of HumRRO's work is classified, and Elliott said he was rather generally against a university's doing secret research. He added, however, that "rigid exclusion of all classified research is debatable." Asked whether he believed HumRRO was an advantage or disadvantage to the university, Elliott replied, "There are arguments on both sides."

In contrast to HumRRO's hard-nosed training activities, American University's Center for Research in Social Systems (CRESS) goes in for deeper stuff. Under its former name, SORO (Special Operations Research Office), it launched in 1965 a $1.5 million annual operation called "Project Camelot." It was the bad publicity connected with this that caused it to change its name. The Defense Department had decided at the time that it didn't know enough about the ethnic and other motivational factors involved in the causation and conduct of small wars, and SORO's mission was to establish a research project aimed at building a generalized model of a developing society. The idea was to be able to identify social breakdowns before they actually happened and the communists had taken advantage of them, while at the same time providing information about what kinds of action could be taken to foster constructive change with a degree of relative order and stability. Put bluntly, the Army had taken upon itself to develop a foreign policy to manipulate small poor countries.

Camelot was subcontracted to a number of well-known social scientists at Berkeley, MIT, Princeton and the University of Michigan, among others. One of SORO's men was in Chile, looking around to see whether that country might not usefully be made the guinea pig for the study, and in the process of trying to rope in some of the local scholars, word leaked to the press. This created a furor in the United States, ruined the cover of the project, forced its cancellation and brought on hearings before the Congress.

After Camelot, SORO changed its name to CRESS but kept on with the same sort of work. CRESS has its headquarters in Washington, a few blocks away from the campus of American University. There are no joint appointments between the American University faculty and the CRESS staff, but CRESS people are treated as faculty members, with such benefits as health care, membership in the eating club and free tuition. While the university is given a veto over CRESS projects, this has rarely been invoked, and in practice, CRESS is left alone to pursue its Army mission—which is "to conduct empirical and theoretical research, and provide information storage, retrieval and analysis services with a multidisciplinary orientation on social and cultural problems related to foreign areas of relevance to U.S. government programs."

What precisely does this mean? In 1964 CRESS, then

SORO, published a work entitled "Witchcraft, Sorcery, Magic and other Psychological Phenomena and Their Implications on Military and Paramilitary Operations in the Congo." Friendly African troops have been a bother, since witch doctors employed by the enemy persuade them that their magic turns bullets to water. The soldiers throw down their arms and rush into the enemy fire. CRESS said this sort of thing could be averted if the Army first gathered reliable intelligence, and then counterinsurgency planners could "concoct medicines and other devices within the superstitious framework of the target group, with which to neutralize and overpower the magic spells cast by insurgent witch-doctors."

CRESS has made numerous other interesting research studies, including several on "word-of-mouth communications" in Thailand and China, the use of propaganda leaflets during a war, casebooks on twenty-three revolutions in seven major geographic areas, rural violence in Colombia, and so on. During 1966 CRESS published an advanced research paper called "Combating Subversively Manipulated Civil Disturbances," which suggested that police might best handle riots in the United States by infiltrating "subversive" groups with intelligence agents, and when it came to rioting crowds, they could do things like send electric shocks through streams of water, turn on sound projectors that produced intolerable noises, shine spotlights in the rioters' eyes, thereby temporarily destroying their vision, and shoot tranquilizers at them. Like much of the rest of CRESS's research, this material was a second-hand job, stolen from *Ordnance Magazine* and written by an ex-member of the military police.

Then there is a series of "Intercultural Communications Guides," originally known as "Psychological Operations Handbooks," which identifies different groups in twenty-four countries and summarizes their attitudes toward the United States. "Each group is assessed for its susceptibility to persuasion, its effectiveness or influence within its own society and its potential for furthering the interest of the United Staes under various conditions. In addition, each study contains the latest available data on communications facilities within the country and on cultural factors relevant to communication."

Occasional papers include "Psychological Operations Vulnerabilities of the Soviet Union," also known as EXPLOIT-USSR, written in 1964 (this project was commonly called "Operation Doorstop" until China appeared on the scene when the heading of the paper was changed to read EXPLOIT-CHINA); pamphlets on political influence of students in Latin America in 1967 and an examination in 1967 of the Christian Democrats there. At the time, the CIA was attempting to maneuver the Christian Democrats under the cover of the National Students Association.

CRESS operates two branch offices in addition to its headquarters in Washington. One is at the John F. Kennedy Special Warfare Center at Fort Bragg, where the Rangers get their training. The other is in Korea, where the Army is at work on civic-action programs. In 1963 the center opened an office at the U.S. Army Command in the Canal Zone, but there wasn't enough work for the staff and it was closed down a year and a half later. Although much of CRESS's research is on insurgency and counterinsurgency techniques in Vietnam, it hasn't maintained an office there, but instead sends out teams of experts from time to time to Vietnam and other parts of Southeast Asia.

While a number of social scientists have recently promised to stop meddling in the affairs of foreign countries, these projects still go on. The University of California at Berkeley runs a Himalayan Border Countries Project, originally funded by the Ford Foundation. Professor Robert A. Scalapino, an advisor to the State Department and supporter of the Administration's policies in Vietnam, was instrumental in switching the Himalayan research from Ford to the Advanced Research Projects Agency of the Pentagon, where it was awarded a

$282,000 contract. The Berkeley professors maintain a research station in Nepal, and they have been investigating communism in the Himalayan areas, reporting back on the defense capabilities of the state of Sikkim, and the Northeast Frontier Agency of India. Gordon P. Means, one of the researchers, went to Nagaland. The progress report describes his mission: "Professor Means has projected a multifaceted research program on various aspects of political development in Nagaland, all of which may be pursued concurrently if field work in the area for an extensive period proves feasible in 1968/1969. These projects fall into three general categories:

(a) A political socialization study of primary and secondary schoolchildren in a select number of communities in Nagaland.

(b) A study of the development of political parties and political leadership in Nagaland, based on interviews with key individuals in the Nagaland Legislative Assembly, the collection of biographical data on Naga leaders, the examination of political recruitment patterns, and an analysis of the basic issues which activate Nagaland politics.

(c) An investigation of elite communication patterns in Nagaland, and particularly between the 'underground' (i.e., rebel Naga leaders) and the 'overground' (official Naga leaders).

"Obviously there is considerable variation in the sensitivity of these three programs, and the present plan is to proceed with the first and then undertake the other two only if and when these seem feasible."

Thus the professors go to Nagaland, with a cover of studying schoolchildren, in hopes of gathering intelligence on the underground.

Gerald D. Berreman, a Berkeley professor who had worked on the Himalayan research, quit the project when he discovered it was financed by the Pentagon. In a letter of resignation, Berreman said: "These agencies [Defense agencies] are not disinterested patrons of scholarship nor

of furtherance of an understanding of the Himalayan peo-
ples and nations. I can imagine only one reason for their
support of this project: To provide information useful in
the application of force, including violence and intrigue,
to enforce, support or initiate policies in the Himalayan
region which are favored by the Administration—policies
such as 'containing' or pushing back China, 'freeing'
Tibet, supporting insurgency in Tibet, supporting counterinsurgency in northeastern India, supporting strongly
pro-American elements throughout this region. I want no
part of this. I feel a positive obligation to oppose it."

While a university's contribution to the design and manufacture of bombs, missiles and other sorts of military
hardware is meant to be taken rather seriously, the contributions of the social scientists in concocting grandoise
schemes for psychological warfare are generally viewed
more as a civilian employment scheme rather than making any sort of real contribution to the military. The main
exception to this is the Institute for Defense Analysis, a
consortium of eleven universities, based in Arlington, Virginia, which when McNamara was Secretary of Defense
seemed to have had some real influence.

James R. Killian, Jr., chairman of the board of MIT,
put together IDA in 1959. MIT had been asked by
Charles Wilson, then the Secretary of Defense, to evaluate our weapons systems, but Killian felt that MIT was
already enough involved with the Defense Department,
and so he proposed that instead of MIT's taking on the
job alone, he would try to found a consortium of universities. Killian got five schools to go along: Case Institute
of Technology, MIT, Stanford, Tulane and California Institute of Technology. The Ford Foundation made a grant
of $500,000, and Killian became the first chairman of the
board of the Institute for Defense Analysis. Later the
University of California, Michigan, Penn State, Princeton,
Columbia, Chicago and Illinois joined the group. The institute's main headquarters is in Washington. IDA also

maintains a code-breaking center at Princeton, where it can get expert help from that university's faculty. This center is linked to the National Security Agency.

The problem, then and now, was to inveigle bright university scientists to come into the Defense Department, either as consultants or for short stints on various projects, without tedium of the civil service or the low-pay scale of government work. In addition, IDA was to set up an organization that would in some measure give the Secretary of Defense, through his director of research and development, a variety of contingency reports, including studies on tactical nuclear weapons in Southeast Asia.

The affairs of the institute are directed by a board of trustees consisting of the officers of sponsoring universities. The annual reports are couched in language that attempts to show how the university provides the technical innovation for problem-solving in the real world for Defense-oriented missions, and is accompanied by pictures of charming old buildings on the campuses of the sponsoring institutions. In fact, IDA's headquarters is in a ghastly new building located on a muddy lot down the road from the Pentagon. Armed guards stand at the elevators, and to get inside, one goes to a receptionist, who says cheerfully, "Will this be a classified or an unclassified visit?" She then calls upstairs, arranges for an escort, then hands out a card that says in red letters, "Escort Required." Once inside the secured area, which consists of seven out of the building's ten floors, all one sees is a stream of Ivy League types with security-clearance passes around their necks, locking and unlocking their safes.

Norman L. Christeller, the director of IDA's operations, makes it perfectly clear that the universities have nothing whatever to do with the administration of the place, nor is there any real exchange of staffs. IDA's staff totals 625 people, only twelve of whom were on leave from their universities. Christeller pointed out, however, that the universities were of some help to IDA. For one

thing, the presidents or deans of the sponsoring schools
do help recruit personnel. If IDA has some kind of difficult problem it wants help with, it can call up a university
and be put in touch with someone who can answer the
question.

The only continuing link to the universities seems to be
through the Jason program, which is meant to lure some
of the younger, brighter scientists, especially physicists,
into thinking about Defense problems. This division now
includes thirty to forty men, who have agreed to spend
one fifth of their university time with IDA. In addition,
they spend two months in the summer at special workshops. A consultant to IDA can make up to $200 a day
plus travel and incidental expenses. The members of
Jason originally were heavily oriented around Princeton,
where the division director is employed, but they also
come from Yale, Harvard and Columbia.

In recent years there have been signs that the people
who work for IDA have become bored with military
planning, and like all other military think tanks, they
want to move into civilian programs such as operations
analyses for the poverty program, studies for the National
Crime Commission about using computers to improve police efficiency, and come up with enterprising new ideas
for crowd control. This involves an itching powder, sticky
blobs to glue rioters together, chemical agents, mechani-
cally spread sticky strings, bands of adhesives which
might slow the movement of the crowd by linking people
together or to themselves, foam generators which lead to
"psychological distress through loss of contact with the
environment," and tranquilizing darts. But civilian work
didn't really catch on at IDA, and many of the people
who were interested in it have left.

The universities that sponsor IDA claim it is independent, which is their rationale for belonging. This is self-
serving nonsense. In 1967 IDA was hired by the Federal
Aviation Agency to make a study of the effect of the pro-

posed supersonic transport program on balance of payments. At that time the aircraft industry, which heavily influences both the FAA and the Air Force, was pushing for the SST (Supersonic transport plane), and one of the arguments was that it would be able to shuttle more foreign tourists to the United States, where they would spend a lot of money. IDA examined the possibilities and concluded that this would not at all be the case, and if anything, the U.S. balance of payments would be worsened by making the plane. This report was turned over to the FAA, which, with a congressional debate pending, hid it from view. IDA made no move to get the study into the open. Had it done so, congressional opinion might well have swung the other way. In a very elemental way, the institute violated every one of the universities' lofty statements about free publication, and in this completely unclassified area, lined up with the aircraft industry.

In the fall of 1967 the Princeton chapter of the Students for a Democratic Society attacked Princeton's involvement with IDA, asking that Goheen resign from IDA's board of trustees, and that the university drop its membership and cease to house the communications division. By way of reply, Goheen defended Princeton's relationship with the IDA declaring that the government should have access to the latest and best scientific thinking.

SDS asked for, but was refused, a hearing before the board of trustees. It then staged a sit-down on the IDA laboratory steps, keeping the employees from going to work. The demonstrators were subsequently arrested and fined. Goheen then called a meeting of the university community, during which he defended Princeton's membership in IDA. Professor John Tukey, the statistics professor, supported him. He said, "If you believe that it is good for the government to get the best advice it can, whether or not it follows it, then you should protect the status of IDA." Tukey ought to know, he gives the government the best advice he can, as associate director of the Bell Telephone Laboratories.

Following several student protests against those universities belonging to IDA, the member schools undertook a series of intricate maneuvers last spring to make it appear as if they were quitting the organization. First, the University of Chicago announced it was severing ties with the institute and therefore would no longer appoint a trustee. But this does not mean that professors at the university will stop working for IDA, and as a spokesman at the institute slyly suggested, while Chicago may not appoint a trustee to IDA, IDA might well appoint its own trustee at the University of Chicago. The University of Michigan said it was cutting ties, but that it would continue to appoint some prominent educator to the IDA board. This person would represent himself and not the university. Finally, in June, all the member universities adopted this dodge. They agreed to abandon formal institutional sponsorship, and instead send along representatives as individuals.

Even if the war research for the Pentagon and the shadow liberal government within the CIA were not especially important in terms of the results, these endeavors demonstrated how comfortable it was for a university as an institution, and for professors as individuals, to work through a closed system of government. There is little real interest in the universities in altering their fundamental relationship with the Defense Department. Those who run the universities know, however, that they need to preserve at all costs the myth of their independence from government. Running through all of the ideological arguments devised for taking the cash from the Pentagon are the vague strains of a blend of scientism and patriotism: a government needs to be served by the dispassionate knowledge which only a few experts are capable of dispensing.

There is no such thing as dispassionate knowledge that

can be requisitioned on demand to serve the interests of entrenched groups like the military. It is too late for the myth. The universities were bought by the Pentagon long ago.

7. Multiversity, Inc.

With 90,000 students, a budget of nearly $1 billion and nine campuses, the University of California is the largest dummy corporation in the world. It functions as a university, but more nearly resembles a supra-government through which the private interests that reflect the diverse economy of the country's biggest state control California. Wherever the entrenched interests of California are threatened—in agriculture, land exploitation, cheap labor or ammunition—the University of California rises to their defense.

This empire is governed by twenty-three regents, six of them politicians or state officials, the remainder appointed for six-year terms by the governor. They meet in small committees or subcommittees, using the university as banker-broker.

In exchange for sufficient government funds to enable California to become the chief munitions dump in the nation, the university built the H bomb. When the regents got interested in constructing new towns in the arid southern part of the state, the university dispatched professors and students to Irvine to start a new campus. By purchasing electricity for the Berkeley campus from public sources the university would have saved the state's taxpayers some $20 million, but then that would have been an affront to the interests of the Pacific Gas & Electric Company. The profits of the agribusiness were threatened when the United States Department of Labor suggested that it was wrong to import Mexican braceros for stoop labor at low wages. University economists were sent scurrying around the state to persuade the populace that should the importation of braceros be stopped, the whole of California agriculture would be ruined.

As befits a supra-government, the university receives foreign emissaries, maintains legations around the world, and negotiates directly with the federal government in Washington, where the university has two wholly owned subsidiaries—the Atomic Energy Commission and the Directorate of Defense Research and Engineering in the Pentagon. Glenn Seaborg, chairman of the AEC, was chancellor at Berkeley, and it is through the commission that the university draws out money for work on the bomb. Even more important than the chairman of the AEC, the director of Defense Research and Engineering sets future armaments priorities for the whole defense establishment, and then spends the money to put projects in motion. John Foster, the current director, came from the Radiation Laboratory as did his two predecessors. Nearly half of all the government's expenditures for research at universities goes to California, and directors of these two subsidiaries are there to make sure things stay that way.

Industry's connections to the University of California are not neglected either: Dr. Franklin Murphy, until recently the chancellor at UCLA, was emissary to the Ford Motor Company whose biggest market is in California. He also functioned as the university's general ambassador to Latin America, where California agribusiness interests export pesticides and mechanized equipment; Roger Heyns, the chancellor at Berkeley, is the local representative on the board of Hunt Foods, whose chairman, Norton Simon, is a regent; Chancellor Emil M. Mrak of the barnyard campus at Davis is the man the tin-can companies look to for new processing techniques. It was at the Davis campus that farm experts speedily developed a tomato picker once the government cut off the bracero program. Research and experimentation was all accomplished with the public's money and the final product given away to agribusiness interests.

Although the University of California is almost entirely dependent upon public funds, it never has published a portfolio to show where the money is invested. According to the treasurer, Owsley Hammond, this is because they don't wish to give speculators any opportunity to influence university holdings. Regent Simon, who sits on the investments committee, said that even he didn't know what was going on with the money and because the committee rarely held meetings it is difficult to find out where it is invested.

Within the banker-broker-arrangements setup and perpetuated by the regents a battle is constantly being waged to see which of the interests can control the whole. It is generally believed that the power of the regents lies with two men. One is Edwin Pauley, a hulking old man who ran Harry Truman's campaign in 1948 and is big in oil in the southern part of the state. The other is Edward Carter, the neat, humorless chairman of Broadway-Hale, the large western department store chain. Theodore Meyer is a San Francisco lawyer who works for Carter. He was made head of something called the Mechanics Institute, an office which under state law automatically made him a regent. From there he quickly rose to become chairman.

The regents gather once a month for a public business meeting, but even then one needs a pass to get by the armed police who stand in front of the door to the conference room. Nothing much goes on at these dreary affairs, aside from petty quarreling among the politicians. Jesse Unruh, the Democratic state boss, uses the monthly meetings as a way to get a favorable press by taunting Governor Reagan who is an ex-officio regent. Simon sometimes quarrels with Pauley over the disposition of the investment reports. And there is chit-chat about communists, perverts and other freaks. Mrs. Randolph A. Hearst is concerned about dope and likes to talk about that and orgies. She disapproves of both.

If the open meetings of the regents are hopeless, the executive sessions of the committees where the real business goes on are closed to the public. The minutes are not given out, if indeed they are even kept. So there is no real way to follow how the company works. Still, one need not go far afield to find of evidences of the "uses of the university," as former president Dr. Clark Kerr refers to them.

Thus, in the late 1950's, Cadet Hand, a marine biologist at the Berkeley campus, interested the university in constructing a marine biological laboratory at Bodega Head, a promontory surrounded by coves full of interesting aquatic life, a few miles up the coast from San Francisco. The idea seems to have been well received, since the university could well use such a laboratory, and it complemented the state's own plans to turn Bodega Head into a state park. Then, in 1960, the state departments in charge of the project suddenly lost interest, and on inquiring why, the Berkeley scientists were informed that Pacific Gas & Electric Company, had decided to use Bodega Head for a nuclear power station. In the judgment of Glenn T. Seaborg, then the chancellor of the Berkeley campus and now head of the Atomic Energy Commission, and presumably a man who knew something of such things, the plans for an atomic station made it "undesirable to locate a marine laboratory" at Bodega Head. Aside from generally ruining the look of the place, the nuclear plant would dump huge amounts of hot water into the cove, upsetting the aquatic life.

On first receiving news of the electric company's move, the marine biologists were disposed to fight for the lab, but when one of them approached high officials within the university, he was told to forget it. The biologists subsequently sought other sites, but none of them was anywhere near as favorable as Bodega Head, and finally Hand argued that they had better settle for Bodega Head, even if it meant studying dead fish, or else they would completely lose the laboratory. This all turned out very well for Hand because he later got a grant from the AEC to study the effects of the nuclear station on aquatic life.

One of the scientists, Dr. John Nielands, went after the university for not standing up to the power company. Nielands claimed there was a "sticky relationship" between the University of California and Pacific Gas & Electric Company, and that it might be rather embarrassing for the university to oppose the P G & E since James Black, the late chairman of the company, had led the campaign to raise $2.4 million for a university building. More to the point, John Sproul, the attorney for the company, was the son of Gordon Sproul, former president of the university.

The issue was never properly resolved, for the company belatedly discovered that the nuclear power plant would lie too close to a major earthquake fault, and the university built its laboratory.

Whether or not the university really was brought under any direct pressure from P G & E, it is interesting to note that during this period Robert Underhill, then the treasurer of the university, in making an evaluation of the university's stockholdings, had visited with the officials of P G & E. He urged that the stock be held, pointing out that prospects for additional business were rosy because of the proposed facilities at Bodega Head.

While the forces at work in the Bodega Head affair may well have been subtle, there was nothing whatever subtle about the university's dealings with P G & E for electricity. Since 1906 the University of California has purchased electricity for the Berkeley campus from the company. With the Radiation Laboratory engaged in large-scale experiments, the costs had become heavy. In 1967, for instance, the Berkeley campus spent $1.8 million for electricity, with $1 million of that total accounted for by the Radiation Laboratory. In 1957 the total costs for power at Berkeley ran to $400,000.

In 1962 the regents contracted with R. W. Beck Associates, an independent firm of consulting engineers, for a study of the best methods for obtaining electric power for the Berkeley campus. Its report, marked "strictly confidential," argued that the university might save $20 million over ten years on that campus by shifting from P G & E to buying federal power. Governor Pat Brown then wrote to the Secretary of Interior, Stewart Udall, asking him in behalf of the university for an allocation of federal electricity. Udall said he could make the electricity available immediately on a short-term basis, and that both parties could then explore the possibility of getting long-term power for future use.

The difficulty, however, was that federal power lines do not run to Berkeley, but stop at the Central Valley project, fifty miles away. To bring in the cheap electricity, it would be necessary to get P G & E to agree to wheeling it, that is, carry it over the company's lines the remaining distance. P G & E refused to wheel the power, offering instead to reduce rates by $2.5 million over ten years, a fraction of the saving to be had from use of the federal lines. The university could have put pressure on the power company, since the Atomic Energy Commission foots the bill for the Radiation Laboratory, or might have joined forces with the city of Berkeley, which was then contemplating building electricity lines in order to get the less expensive federal power, or it could well have built lines of its own. Instead the regents and administrators argued that things would be simpler to go along with P G & E, and signed a new contract with the company spending the $20 million.

The grandest business in California is building new towns in the arid southern part of the state. Almost any decent businessman has his finger in this pot, and the regents of the university stand foremost among them. The Chandlers' *Times-Mirror* interests build new towns, and Edwin Pauley, the oil man, has promised to build some.

The only problem these entrepreneurs face is to bring in cheap water. Californians look after their own, and Governor Pat Brown persuaded the legislature to approve the building of an enormous aqueduct from the San Francisco Bay area, in the northern part of the state, south past Los Angeles to the desert. The result of this scheme would be to reduce the water levels in the Bay area and allow the salty bay water to creep up into the northern delta. Any water shortage in the north means incurring the enormous expense of bringing in federal water from the Northwest.

Thus the businessmen in the south can get cheap water for their housing development, paid for by the taxpayers, most of whom live in the cities.

To make a new town a sure bet, one needs to import people in wholesale numbers. Perhaps the easiest and quickest way to graft a new community onto the countryside is to bring in a university, with its built-in consumer community of professors and students. This is what the Irvine Company had in mind in 1959 when it offered the University of California one thousand acres in the midst of its huge ranch in Orange County, just south of Los Angeles. The Irvine ranch covers some 140 square miles, or 20 percent of the county, stretching from the ocean back into the hills, and supporting diverse agricultural crops and cattle. It was assembled by the Irvine family from old Spanish land grants, and when the last owner, James Irvine, Jr., died in 1947 he split up the land. He gave 49 percent of the stock of this enterprise to different members of the family, and the other 51 percent to the Irvine Foundation, a charitable organization, one of the trustees of which was Edward Carter, the department-store man and regent of the university.

The origins of the complex relationship between the University of California and the company began when the company announced it would turn the ranch into a new city, planned by the well-known architect William Pereira. The university needed a new campus in the bulging Los Angeles suburbs, and this seemed an altogether generous offer. From the company's point of view it was a shrewd move as well, for the campus, with its faculty, students and various professional staffs, would accomplish several things at once. It would produce the people to live in houses the company would build, create a demand for goods and services that could be met by company-built shopping centers and bring in the sort of light industry, and research and development business, which would be drawn to Orange County because of its climate, the proximity of the beaches and nearness to the university.

The regents actually signed a tentative agreement with the Irvine Company in March of 1959, a few days after Arthur McFadden's term as a regent expired. At the time, McFadden was president of the Irvine Company.

Orange County is the most conservative part of California, and the Irvines sought to perpetuate their control by leasing their land instead of selling it. Leases do not produce money over the short term, but over a long period, the enterprise would flourish, because the company, in effect, would own the land and let the tenants develop it for them. This immediately raised the question of whether the university should as a public institution contribute to a new sort of feudal enterprise. More important, the university was concerned because of the restrictive policies of the company, fearing that faculty members, especially Jews and Negroes, might have a difficult time settling down around the campus. On the insistence of several regents, the company agreed to a non-discriminatory clause which would cover faculty and staff housing. Doubts still lingered, and on seeking a more detailed clarification of the lease procedures, the regents were rebuffed. Charles S. Thomas, who succeeded McFadden as president of the Irvine Company and was former Secretary of the Navy under President Eisenhower, told them, "As long as there is the right of private ownership, an owner might have some valid reason, other than race, color or creed, whereby he could properly have some reasonable control over lease assignment." A resident of the Irvine development remembered that before he was permitted to rent a home on land leased from the company, the real estate agent asked that he fill out a special form, which sought to determine what church he belonged to and whether he considered himself to be a person of high moral standards, these apparently being some of the other criteria to which Thomas alluded.

On July 22, 1960, the regents formally thanked the Irvine Company for the gift of 1,000 acres and set into the record an agreement stating that an adjacent "inclusion" area for housing would consist of 660 acres to be appraised as of July 1, 1960. The company proposed to develop the faculty housing under some plan agreeable to both the university and itself, and failing in this endeavor, the university could then exercise an option to purchase outright the land in the inclusion area.

The company was to produce a plan by the fall of 1960, but for three years it continued to ask for and receive extensions. Apparently it was never able to produce the development money for the scheme. These delays, however, worked to the Irvines' advantage, for as the university's plans for the new campus went ahead, the price of the neighboring land went up. To make matters more confused, the university also hired Pereira as its own architect.

The negotiations dragged along. By May 1, 1961, Robert Underhill reported to the regents that they could have the land for $4000 per acre minimum, or a total of $2.6 million. Four days later, on May 5, 1961, Underhill reported in a second memorandum that he had just talked with Loyal McLaren of the Irvine Company, who apparently convinced him "that while the appraisal date was twenty-two days prior to the agreement, the appraisers felt that matters were so far along and so many tentative understandings had been made that it seemed certain the site would be formally chosen within a few days to that time, and they regarded the choice as already in effect. Under the circumstances, they feel that a $6000 figure is appropriate if not on the conservative side." Thus within the space of three days the price for the deal rose by one third to $3.9 million, and the agreed-upon appraisal went out the window. Still nothing was concluded, and by March 22, 1962, almost a full year later, President Kerr had injected himself into the negotiations. The minutes record his surprise at finding the price, which he understood to be set at $4000 per acre, had suddenly risen to $6000 an acre. Now both the company and the university made separate appraisals, based supposedly on what the land could have sold for on July 1, 1960. The company said the land was worth nearly $10,000 an acre on that date, while the university appraiser, who based his estimates largely on sales made after the appraisal date, said it was worth $7000 an acre.

Appraising is not an especially scientific art, and the university had not taken the usual precaution of having two estimates made, which then could be balanced one against the other. As it was, the appraiser's evaluation was based on sales of land that were made two years after the appraisal date. At any rate, judging the value of the Irvine land would be especially difficult since for years a relative of the family had held a job as county appraiser, and according to one report, although most people paid 50 percent of the appraised value in taxes, the Irvines were paying two to three percent for the land, doubtless because they used it for cattle-grazing purposes. A second independent appraisal made at this time showed that the land was worth $3000 an acre, at the most, $4000. Finally, in October of 1963, Kerr, who had expressed such shock at the increased price, negotiated the final deal, which he regarded as "favorable to the university." Under this scheme, the university agreed to pay $6500 an acre for 510 acres (the company had wanted to get back land that had a sea view, which they could lease at double the price for land that did not), or more money for less land. The regents subsequently approved the plan, thereby having neatly talked themselves out of 150 choice acres and over $1 million. Thus, in exchange for

1000 free acres, the Irvines established the base for a new city, and holding up the university on a side deal, got some quick cash for further development.

At the time there was some speculation over the role of Edward Carter, the chairman of Broadway-Hale and a trustee of the Irvine Foundation as well as a regent. He was building a new department store just down the street from the Irvine campus, and there was some question as to whether he could be entirely impartial in the matter. However, Carter insists he took special pains to avoid any possibility of conflict of interest, making sure not to participate in discussions with the regents on the deal.

By virtue of the fact that the University of California is a land grant institution, it operates two campuses (Davis and Riverside) devoted to agricultural research, as well as an elaborate network of 500-odd agricultural extension workers, who at one time worked closely with small farmers, showing them how to get more production out of the land. In addition, the university acts as the state's scientific advisor on pesticides, testing new chemicals and advising whether they are safe and efficacious; if they are, the university distributes the information to the extension agents. But as it turns out, the pesticide research, supposedly carried on by the scientists at the University of California, is in fact often undertaken by representatives of the chemical companies who want to sell new pesticides. Thus a university extension agent in Fresno told a visiting student how research was done. He had recently received a $70,000 grant from four chemical companies that wanted to test new pesticides for use against the lygus worm and bollworm, two cotton pests. The university often takes on this sort of industry-sponsored project, but in this case the actual research in the field, which consisted of counting the bugs before and after the spraying, was to be done by chemical company employees, which according to the farm advisors was not an unusual procedure. The chemical company thus used the university as a façade behind which they tested and marketed their new products.

Through its agricultural divisions, the university always has been associated with the growers' crude campaign to continue the use of braceros, the Mexican laborers who are hauled across the border and paid a pittance to harvest crops. Willard Wirtz, the Secretary of Labor, sharply curtailed the importation of braceros in 1964.

But in 1956, when this issue was not popular, the National Institutes of Health financed a study undertaken by Henry Anderson and some of his associates at the Public Health School on the Berkeley campus. Anderson's observations of the conditions of the Mexicans working in the field led to a report to the American Friends Service Committee, which argued that there was no use just tinkering with the bracero system, that it wreaked such havoc on the people who went through it that it must be "extricated, root and branch." This began a round of troubles, first with the head of the California Department of Employment, and later with the local U.S. Labor Department officials, who wrote Anderson, demanding to know who he thought he was, and said he would have to produce the "evidence" to back up his "charges." Anderson replied that he was not charging anybody with anything, but that he had come to his conclusion after personally watching conditions in the field—that the bracero system was horrible and ought to be done away with. Anderson said in 1958, "I received a telephone call from Berkeley. The School of Public Health had been told by top university officials that the field work was to stop immediately. I was told that I could 'write up' the data already in hand, if I wished, but that I was to conduct no more interviews, or have any other contact with the public. My interviewers were discharged. The U.S. Department of Labor was informed that I would not be returning to its reception centers." Anderson later learned that the government agencies had pressured the local Farm Bureau office, which in turn had called up Harry Wellman, a university vice-president and agriculturist; the bureau promised to ask nasty questions when the university came up for funds in the legislature. Anderson later wrote up his findings, but the faculty advisory committee dismissed them out of hand as having wandered too far from the field of health, and were too "controversial" and shoddy. Anderson continued to snipe at the university over the handling of the matter, and following a radio broadcast over Station KPFA, a group of concerned professors from the Academic Freedom Committee of the Faculty Senate made an investigation. In their report they confirmed that the university had indeed buckled to pressure from the U.S. Labor Department in calling off the study, but nonetheless concluded blandly, ". . . the charge of a violation of academic freedom in connection with Mr. Anderson's project is without foundation."

By the spring of 1964 the pressure had mounted against the Labor Department to cut out the importation of braceros, and after a conference with Undersecretary of Labor John Henning, Governor Brown engaged the University of California to make two studies. The Gianni Foundation at Berkeley, always loyal to the barnyard people, reported on the needs and supply of agricultural labor. UCLA looked into the availability of labor supply should the program be ended. Eric Thor, an agricultural economist who made the Gianni report, concluded that foreign workers were badly needed, and if they were to be eliminated, the state's economy would be plunged into ruin. Thor said there was a shortage of farm workers nationally (yet according to the Department of Labor figures for that time, there were 1.4 million unemployed farm workers). Thor pointed out that unemployed workers in the city would not leave their unemployment benefits for stoop labor on the farms, which was perfectly obvious, the average weekly wage for hard labor, sunup to sundown, being about $55 per week. The UCLA report, made by Fred Schmidt of the Institute of Industrial Relations, said that if they were decently paid and given civilized treatment, half of the 660 unemployed people he had interviewed in Los Angeles would take jobs in the field, although only one sixth of that total said they would take the work at the going wage of $55 a week. Schmidt's report was greeted by the farmers as a "blueprint for disaster for California agriculture." Dr. Thor, heralded as the most knowledgeable and informed man in California, was then sent around the state—tearing up the UCLA study and urging the farmers to lobby for continuance of the bracero program.

When I was in California in the fall of 1967, Cesar Chavez, leader of the farm workers' organization, was in the midst of his campaign to organize farm workers into a union. I asked Dr. Ivan Hinderaker, the political scientist who is chancellor of the Riverside campus, the southern agricultural center, how he viewed the unionizing of farm workers; Dr. Hinderaker said he was a political scientist and really didn't know much about the subject. Being uninformed, he didn't have any opinions. Then I asked Dr. Aldrich, the chancellor at Irvine who had been chancellor of Riverside and who sat on a U.S. Labor Department panel which had worked out a scheme to reduce the number of braceros, how he viewed the unionizing effort; Aldrich said he just didn't know. When I brought up the subject of braceros with Dr. Mrak, the outspoken chancellor at the Davis campus, he said it was his opinion that ending importation of braceros was like cutting out a useful AID program for Mexicans, leaving them all lying around with little to do.

Elias H. Tuma, an economist at Davis, has an idea for getting around the whole mess. Tuma suggests bringing in a number of young people from underdeveloped countries to work on California farms, thereby providing the foreigners with experience in advanced American farm methods, and providing the California growers with a manpower pool in peak harvest months.

If the University of California begins to look like the

dummy behind which the different interest groups in California maneuver, Stanford, another well-known university, located several miles south of San Francisco at Palo Alto, is the center for quite another sort of intellectual endeavor. It is designing a foreign policy so that Americans can dominate the Pacific Basin.

At the center of this enterprise was Ernest C. Arbuckle, who until 1968 was dean of the Stanford Business School and chairman of the board of the university's big research subsidiary, the Stanford Research Institute (SRI). In 1957 Arbuckle quit a post as vice-president of W. R. Grace & Company to take the Stanford position. He left Stanford in 1968 to become chairman of the Wells-Fargo Bank, the third largest bank in California. When Arbuckle came to Stanford he used the university to further the interests of several business enterprises. The deals between the companies and the university got pretty tangled. And an outline of the far-flung operation is instructive.

Along with Alf E. Brandin, the university's vice-president for business affairs, Arbuckle, then at Stanford, was a director of the Utah Construction and Mining Company. The president of that company, Edmund W. Littlefield, was a prominent Stanford trustee. Among its other enterprises, Utah Mining owns 50 percent in the Marcona Mining Company, which mines iron ore in Peru. Through its various subsidiaries, Marcona builds ships in Japan, then uses them to haul the iron ore from Peru and Australia (where Utah has another joint venture), out to Japan, where the raw ore is manufactured. Utah also is involved in Thailand, where it constructs B-52 bases.

Arbuckle is also a director of Castle & Cook, whose president, Malcolm MacNaughton, sits on the board of trustees of the Stanford Research Institute. Castle & Cook owns Dole, the pineapple company, which in 1967 opened a pineapple-processing plant in the Philippines. In Japan, Dole operates two joint ventures with the Japanese, and sells its Philippine bananas through a Japanese trading company. In addition, it controls a glass-making firm in the Philippines and is looking around to expand this business among the Pacific nations. Castle & Cook own terminals in harbors, and is seeking to establish through joint ventures a shipping company that can make the mainland-to-Hawaii run. In addition, it owns an interest in the Thai-American Steel Works Company, which makes steel pipe in Bangkok.

On the board of Castle & Cook sat George G. Montgomery, who was chairman of the Kern County Land Company, another firm where Arbuckle is a director. Montgomery was also a member of the Stanford Business School advisory council, and was on the board of the Hoover Institution of War, Revolution and Peace. Kern County owns vast tracts of agricultural land, prospects for gas and oil, and has a gas venture in Australia. It also owns various manufacturing subsidiaries, among them Watkins-Johnson, begun by a former Stanford professor and located in the research park run by Stanford University. Occidental Petroleum made a bid to buy out Kern County, but Arbuckle remembers, they (Kern County) did not much care for Occidental, and turned instead to Gardner Symonds, another Stanford trustee and chairman of Tenneco. Tenneco obliged, upping the merger price by $10 a share, and Kern County leaped at the deal.

In his capacity as dean of the business school and chairman of the board of SRI, Arbuckle was able to complement and extend these various other interests. Thus, in 1963, Stanford sent a team of professors to Peru to lay the groundwork for establishing a new business school, which was to be run by a Stanford professor who was a former vice-president of W. R. Grace & Company's Latin-American operations. In its first two years Grace, Marcona Mining and Ralston Purina were the main companies hiring the graduates of ESAN, as the school was called. Marcona, along with others, sponsored an exchange program whereby professors from Peru were sent to Stanford to learn new business techniques. Then the

Peace Corps contracted with the Stanford Business School to train thirty-five to forty American graduates of business schools to go down to Peru and help the Peruvians improve the management of small businesses and co-operatives. The idea was that the program also was meant to give the Americans some experience in Latin America, and Arbuckle remembers that Marcona was so enthused about the Peace Corps volunteers that it rushed to hire them. Frank K. Shallenberger, a marketing professor at the business school, was in charge of the affair, which he hawked as a travel tour: "There is a great, big, wonderful, exciting, turbulent world out there and it's going places, but you can't feel it, you can't appreciate it, you can't understand it, unless you go out and see it for yourself . . . you get the great thrill of being in tune, of being a participant instead of an observer, of playing a significant part in the greatest drama of the twentieth century, in mankind's greatest achievement, the development of the underdeveloped world."

Wherever Arbuckle and his business friends go in the Pacific, they tow Stanford Research Institute along behind for publicity. Thus SRI sponsored a conference to buoy business leaders in Sydney, where a message from the President was read. At that conference there was a call for a similar conference in Djakarta, where Cal Tex, an American oil company, had just set up operations, and SRI rushed off there to run a convention publicizing the trade possibilities in Indonesia. SRI helped launch the Japan-California Association, and Mr. Gibson, the president of the institute, set up the Pacific Basin Conference. This venture turned out rather well, since no sooner had SRI set it up, than it hired SRI to perform research. When Dole went into the Philippines, SRI moved in right behind to establish a branch office. With Utah Mining, Castle & Cook and others hard at work with the Japanese, SRI established joint projects with Nomura Research, a Japanese firm, so it could learn how to run research American-style. Following the Sydney conference,

SRI published a gushing report, which carried a special article that said: "Dramatic developments in the shipments of iron ore across the Pacific from Peru and Australia to Japan are well illustrated by the operation of one company alone—the Marcona Corporation of San Francisco."

While the institute has only recently moved into the business of propagandizing this sort of American adventuring in the Pacific, it always has been strong for defending American economic interests there. Staley, the economist at SRI, is given credit for originating the strategic hamlet program around which Diem formed his ill-fated government. While Utah and the others are involved in selling and manufacturing in Thailand, SRI works on counterinsurgency projects for the Defense Department to keep the communists out. It sought to save South Vietnam from the Reds, through intervention of the aforementioned strategic hamlet plan and also by studies of building Cam Ranh Bay and land reform for AID. The institute has 3000 employees, with branch offices in Pasadena, Huntsville, Irvine, Washington and throughout Europe as well as in Asia.

It is a sad and bitter commentary on Stanford University that while it eagerly mounts publicity schemes for American adventuring around the Pacific, and particularly on the west coast of Latin America, it killed the *Hispanic-American Report,* an unusual magazine which reported on events in Latin America as well as those in Spain and Portugal. Aside from plodding through the CIA's daily compendium of radio broadcast transcripts called Foreign Broadcast Reports, the *Hispanic-American Report* was the sole medium that presented any sort of understandable view of what was happening in Latin America. It was the first publication in this country to discover and publish the plans for the U.S. invasion of the Bay of Pigs, and it described in detail the events that led up to the revolution in Cuba as well as what went on there afterward. The magazine was put together by graduate students under the direction of Ronald Hilton, but the university did not regard producing a magazine of this sort as a proper educational function, and cut the graduate program out from under Hilton, eliminating his staff and bringing to a halt publication of the magazine. Hilton was embittered, and was eventually forced out of his position, but spokesmen in the university still slander him. He has been replaced by John J. Johnson, a Latin-American scholar who refers to himself as a "generalist." He is a consultant to the Rand Corporation, and is well known for his studies of the military in Latin America and other segments of the elites. Johnson does not care to discuss the *Hispanic-American Report,* but he says he opposed its continuance because it took up too much of the students' time. They didn't get any "methodology" out of working for the magazine. And as a historian, Johnson said, he was skeptical of people who wrote up things before they knew what they were talking about. Under the direction of Dr. Johnson, Latin-American students are inquiring into the behavior of the Brazilian legislature.

8. Urb-Coin*

The University of Chicago, like any other institution for social improvement in that city, is a tool of the Daley machine. In recent times Mayor Richard J. Daley has taken to decorating the downtown Loop business center with skyscrapers, marinas, shopping centers, and other symbols of renewed industrial vigor. At the same time he fends off the black hordes. The latter, who account for more than one quarter of the city's 3.5 million population, are kept away from the whites and penned into two enormous oblong ghettos reaching out to the south and west of this business district. The policies of the mayor reflect the prejudices of the ethnic communities—the Irish, Poles, Jews, who don't care to live among the blacks—and these attitudes coincide with those of the businessmen who work with Daley.

To contain the blacks, Chicago operates the world's largest public-housing project, a group of high-rise buildings on the South Side, constructed like a concentration camp so the police can keep a closer eye on the inhabitants within. In recent years the man who runs the Chicago Housing Authority, the public agency which administered this project, was Charles Swibel. Swibel was also president of Marx & Company, which rents slum housing.

* Urb-Coin is a game designed for the Army to teach U.S. Special Forces how to put down insurgencies in Vietnam cities. It is now played by schoolchildren in Boston slums to help them better understand the conditions there.

(It was Swibel who boasted to the newspapers that he had bought two large flophouses as suitable investments for his children.) Housing is segregated in Chicago and so are the schools. In order to keep the blacks from getting out of hand, Chicago maintains an elaborate welfare apparatus and model poverty program to dispense largesse. As always, this type of patrimony fails miserably. After Dr. King's murder there was a bout of rioting, which the police put down with undue gentleness. Daley was incensed, and ordered that in the future they shoot "to kill" arsonists and "to maim" looters. As for looting children, he suggested gassing them.

The blacks once formed a pool of cheap labor for business in and around the city, but those concerns have automated much of the unskilled work, and many businesses have now moved out into the suburbs. The rapid-transit system does not run near the new centers of industry, and since the blacks can't afford automobiles, they are increasingly shut off from work. In the last two decades the black neighborhoods of Chicago have become filled with aimless and desperate people.

More than any other city in America, it has been Chicago that deliberately charted and pursued policies of desolation and ruin. They already have pursued in riot, and if further pursued, as there is every expectation to believe they will be, they promise to reduce the city to rubble.

The policies of the Daley administration are identical with those of the University of Chicago, a highly regarded independent institution which, in fact, is little more than a handmaiden of the machine in the South Side of the city. In all fairness, Mayor Daley actually acts as something of a restraining force on the people who run this university, whose ambition for political control is matched only by their loathing of the poor.

Since the early 1950's the principal function of the University of Chicago has been to rid the predominantly middle-class Jewish section of Hyde Park–Kenwood of the black poor who poured over the border after World War II. Once cleared, the area was meant to be secured by means of federal urban-renewal projects, which, like so many other areas around the country, would replace filthy, high-priced slums with clean, even more expensive efficiency apartments. Recently the university has found it profitable to become an "urban laboratory," a fashionable endeavor among the professors, and to cross over into the nearby black Woodlawn ghetto with teams of social scientists who can study this zoo and bring back reports as to how it can better be contained. Its mission, in short, was to carry out the policies of the city in the southern tier, strengthening the walls around part of the black pen, attempting at the same time to pacify its residents.

After a crime wave in March of 1952, a mass meeting of citizens from Hyde Park–Kenwood was held on the university campus, and this resulted in creating the Committee of Five—headed by Chancellor Lawrence Kimpton, successor of Robert Hutchins—which was supposed to come up with specific ideas about what to do in the neighborhood. The committee lost very little time. It proposed to establish a community group to be called the South East Chicago Commission, and promised to produce plans for rehabilitation and renewal. Julian Levi, a corporation lawyer, whose brother Edward was then dean of the law school and is now president of the university, was made head of the commission. The university helped finance the commission's operations the first year with $15,000, and promised annual contributions of $10,000 from then on. Despite the fact that other community organizations and business groups gave money to the commission, the South East group has always been viewed as an arm of the university.

The object of the plan was very simply to get the poor out of Hyde Park–Kenwood, especially the black poor. The university began by putting $4 million into real estate acquisitions; it hired the city's leading realty firm to handle the properties. But Levi and the staff of the South

East Chicago Commission screened and passed on the applicants. Rossi and Dentler, in their book, *The Politics of Urban Renewal,* report the realtors as saying this helped keep the blacks out. When a speculator bought an apartment house and packed it with blacks, Julian Levi paid him a visit, first threatened to take him to court, and then made a generous offer to buy the place. The commission made copious files of the owners, tenants, crimes on various premises, and to get rid of people it regarded as unsavory, turned the information over to insurance companies, police or landlords.

The Woodlawn Organization, a black community group organized by Saul Alinsky, fought to keep the university from extending its south campus into Woodlawn because it would cause housing to be ripped down. In order to get Alinsky, Levi gave out stories to Chicago papers. Accompanied by the university's public relations man, he took the files of the Industrial Areas Foundation, which employs Alinsky, to the papers, and pointing out that the foundation's support came mainly from Catholics, he sought to expose Alinsky as a pawn of Catholics who used the blacks for their own political ends.

Levi worked hard and successfully to change both state and federal legislation so as to give the University of Chicago, and, indeed, other universities, power for controlling their surrounding neighborhoods. In 1953 he got the Illinois state legislature to amend the state's Neighborhood Redevelopment Corporation Act. This act originally authorized the setting up of a redevelopment corporation to rid a neighborhood of slums, and to do so, it needed to either own or have under option 60 percent of the territory involved. Levi persuaded legislators, however, to conserve run-down neighborhoods, and if the owners of 60 percent of the land agreed, the corporation could have eminent domain over the area. Then Levi led a lobby in the Congress which succeeded in amending the urban renewal statutes, so that, in effect, if the university made any improvements in an area within one mile of the campus that area would become eligible for federal urban renewal treatment at virtually no cost to the city. Usually in urban renewal projects the government pays $2 for every $1 put up by the city, but where education institutions make improvements on their own campuses, the government, under Section 112 of the 1959 housing laws, picks up the city's $1 as well. This gives a university real bargaining power with the city hall.

The success of these programs, in operation for twenty years, is not altogether obvious to a visitor. There is the usual aftermath of urban renewal: some apartments built by Zeckendorf before he went down, a feeble shopping plaza constructed on several levels with stores that all look alike. The once-grand hotels on the lake front are dilapidated. The impoverished blacks in Woodlawn push close up to the barriers constructed by the university. The University of Chicago still spends between $500,000 and $700,000 to pay off-duty Chicago police to patrol the streets as university police. This works out well from the university's point of view, for the man who announces himself as a university policeman can, if circumstance requires, reveal himself as a city cop. The black students bitterly insist that they are stopped routinely after dark by the university police, who demand identification papers.

As in most other places, urban renewal has meant higher rents. In order to obtain three rooms even in university buildings students have to pay as much as $250 a month. Consequently, students and young teaching assistants search for less expensive housing outside the Hyde Park area. One girl student told me that in order to escape the high rents of Hyde Park and the sterile atmosphere of the ladies' dormitory, she and a couple of friends went to Woodlawn to live. Her two friends were raped a week later. On calling the police, the girls found that the police routinely reported such information to the university, which in turn notified the parents, who then insisted that the girls live in a university dormitory. Yet

the girls so loathed the university dormitory, they stopped
reporting attacks and continued living in Woodlawn.

Actually, the move of students outside of Hyde Park
works in the university's favor in an odd sort of way. For
as they go into Woodlawn or down the South Side, they
become a white middle-class force—moving into buildings which the lower-middle-class white ethnic groups fled
as the blacks advanced on them; thus the students provide a barrier between the blacks and the university.

As for the university itself, it has come to resemble an
embattled strategic hamlet. Across its most dangerous exposed southern flank lies a greensward called the Mid-
way, sometimes cynically referred to in Chicago as the
DMZ. One block away from the slums are such university
outposts as: the School of Social Service Administration
which sends into Woodlawn teams of students who, working on federal grants, are supposed to figure out what sort
of education the children there need. The university is
building, with federal funds, a new poverty center, where
Mayor Daley's gang will have local offices, and for its
part, the university will get to study what happens when
the welfare worker meets his client in modern surround-
ings. Next to the university the government is constructing a veterans hospital, which also provides interesting
opportunities for young doctors, giving them a chance to
study new cases. Julian Levi has even changed his mind
about the Woodlawn Organization. Where the University
once fought them, now it seeks instead to manipulate the
group, arranging for financing in hopes that Woodlawn
youngsters will protect Hyde Park–Kenwood citizens
from other youth gangs. The University of Chicago seems
ready to engage in any project for social uplift so long as
it helps whites to maintain control of black neighborhoods.

In 1965 the community decided that a new high school
had to be built. The school then serving Hyde
Park–Kenwood was in Woodlawn, mostly black and

badly overcrowded. At the time Benjamin Willis was school superintendent of the city. Some of his policies were regarded as anti-black. He sided with those who argued for building the new high school within the Hyde Park community. The effect of such a decision would be to develop a good high school in a predominantly white neighborhood, meanwhile leaving the old high school to the blacks, letting it slide further downhill. Another faction urged using the Hyde Park School as a base around which to build an educational park, which would result in attracting more white students, and most importantly, bring to bear the resources of the university (which ran its own private school for faculty children), city and government. But the University of Chicago argued against both ideas, and instead sought to construct with federal funds a research laboratory for education. As a result of the university's lack of position in the fight, the educational park was killed and the small school within Hyde Park was constructed.

The University of Chicago's experiment with urban renewal gave Julian Levi a national reputation, and he flies around to other schools, trying to get them to imitate the Chicago experience before they are overrun in their own setting. He has gone to the University of Pennsylvania, which has an operation not unlike Chicago's. The University of Pennsylvania people in turn have gone to New York and got Mayor John Lindsay excited about the "Philadelphia Story," which is to say the Chicago story, and Lindsay rushed out and started up a series of meetings with university people to see what they might do for New York. Levi has also been to Boston, where he was an advisor to Edward Logue, the urban renewal manager, and he has been to both MIT and Harvard, where he is warmly regarded. "Julian makes me cringe," said one of the Harvard officials. "You know, when he wants to empty a place he'll get an insurance company to cancel its policy, then he'll turn around and get the city to condemn the place because it doesn't have any insurance. We just couldn't get away with that here." MIT already has helped out the city of Cambridge with urban renewal projects under Section 112 of the Housing Act; so has the University of Pennsylvania in Philadelphia. Columbia plans to do so in New York. A look at the university pacification program in Cambridge and New York is instructive.

Harvard and MIT squat at opposite ends of Cambridge, across the Charles River from Boston. The middle of Cambridge looks like any other depressed nineteenth-century New England mill town. The population is fragmented among different ethnic groups, with 15 percent of the families living on less than $3000 a year. From one end Harvard expands toward the center, here and there adding new buildings, cutting off blocks, and buying lavish houses which are resold at cost to attract new faculty members. At the other end MIT is surrounded by a net of prospering research and development companies, which the institute aids by setting into motion urban renewal projects and real estate schemes. The new technical companies create a market for skilled workers, so there is a slow influx of students and young technical workers into the middle of the city, forcing out the working-class types and creating housing pressure.

Both Nathan Pusey, the president of Harvard, and James Killian, chairman of MIT, insist that their institutions stand apart from the politics of Cambridge. In fact, Harvard and MIT grip the opposite ends of a giant pair of pliers, closing in on the obsolescent working-class people who live in the middle of town. This troubles the intellectuals' conscience, and so they devise schemes to train people to work in the technical shops the institutions are creating, as well as plans for shifting them around to make things more comfortable; and most recently they, like their counterparts in Chicago, have found it interesting to preserve part of historic Cambridge as an urban laboratory, a zoo of different sorts of quaint old ethnic types, which they can study, and see what happens when the variables change.

While Pusey insists that Harvard is constructing high-rise buildings instead of impinging further on the city of Cambridge, in fact, there are numerous signs that the university itself speculates in the real estate market. For a long time Harvard had an option to pick up an embalming factory several blocks from the campus and near the city center, a move seemingly out of keeping with Pusey's declarations. Shortly before Harvard picked up the option, a young speculator had appeared and asked if Harvard would not like to buy a strip of houses he had assembled on the periphery of the campus. He was asking an exorbitant price, and observing signs of their hesitancy, he informed the Harvard people that should they not care to take the land themselves, he would use it to build a grand new motel. Harvard bought the houses. But while the speculator enthusiastically discussed how he had bilked Harvard on the deal, the university's operators moved fast into another section of town and started buying on their own.

Citizens' groups complain that when Harvard buys a house, it jacks up the price, and Charles P. Whitlock, assistant to the president for civic affairs, confirms this is so. Prices go up 15 percent, he says, because the city assesses these houses at higher rates. (Citizens' groups claim the increase is more nearly 50 percent.)

Since it is surrounded by industrial buildings, MIT, on the other hand, finds itself in a somewhat different position. From time to time the institute buys these nearby properties and holds them. It tries to pick up possible student housing through a subsidiary called Northgate Company. The favorite trick among real estate speculators is to buy frame houses, rent out rooms and keep jacking the prices. The chances of students' protesting are slight, since they are transient and it is simpler for them to double up and pay the higher rents. Northgate seeks to buy these properties and hold the rents steady. It is MIT's hope that at some future time Northgate can be used as a means for developing low-cost housing for the rest of the community as well. Meanwhile the institute encouraged the development of the Kendall Park urban renewal project, which doesn't provide for housing but instead is built around a new NASA regional office. MIT has another urban renewal project which it runs privately. In the early 1960's it had an opportunity to buy out an old Lever Brothers factory, and after doing so, formed a joint venture with Cabot, Cabot & Forbes to develop this property into Technology Square. MIT rents some of the space for its own use, and the research and development facilities take up most of the rest of it. While the MIT campus still occupies only a small space on the banks of the Charles River, its neighbors fear expansion.

In an effort to hold land prices steady, and provide themselves with land to trade readily, both MIT and Harvard buy and hold property. Thus MIT purchased a United Shoe factory, far away from its own campus near Harvard, then leased it back to the Polaroid Corporation. MIT and Polaroid enjoy a cozy relationship; Killian sits on the Polaroid board, and Edwin Land, the Polaroid president, advises MIT.

While the officials at Harvard and MIT do not engage in the crudities of open political fighting, they nevertheless can be scouted into the open on occasion. MIT was made to show its hand in the "inner belt" case. Since 1948 people in Cambridge and politicians around Massachusetts have quarreled among themselves over where to put a new superhighway, called the "inner belt." The original plan was to run a sort of loop from the center of Boston out through Cambridge, thereby allowing cars to get on and off the several radial highways leading into the metropolis. In addition, the loop could relieve traffic jams in the crowded industrial sections of Boston, and provide a way for cars coming up the coast to get around downtown Boston. By now this scheme is largely unnecessary, since the Massachusetts Turnpike goes into the city. But the state and federal road people, in a trance as usual, can't get the plan out of their minds, and at this writing they were still insisting on pushing through with it. The problem is where the road should go, and basically there are two choices. One plan would have it cut through a dilapidated residential section of eastern Cambridge, with the result that between three to five thousand people would be thrown out of their homes, which would be ripped down. Or it might be run instead through an industrial section, disrupting business.

Neither MIT nor Harvard showed much outward interest in this business so long as the road stayed away from them. But in the heat of one of the political battles on the issue, the city hired an engineering firm, which came up with the idea of running the road down an old railroad track and alongside MIT, knocking out some of its laboratories and, perhaps more importantly, hitting through some of the Polaroid Corporation buildings. This caused near-hysteria at MIT. At a lavish press conference, Killian announced the scheme would cost MIT $80 million in lost labs. He said that while he wasn't qualified to say whether an inner belt was needed or not, he did not want it along the railroad track, which was a polite way of saying he was for running it through people's houses.

This all came to a head in February, 1966, at which time Edward B. Hanify, counsel for the institute, appeared before the Cambridge city council. He pointed out that MIT was the second largest taxpayer in the city and the second largest employer, and had been responsible for contributing to the industrial rebirth of New England, due to the research centers located about its edges. "We all know that we live in times of mortal peril, always on the brink of devastation by those communist powers that seek to crush us by moving ahead of us in scientific techniques." Hanify said, "These nations seek perfection in intricate devices, weaponry, missiles and air power. In this way they confidently expect that they will gain the mastery of space, the domination of the tides and the conquest of the atmosphere. The laboratories and research facilities which this so-called recommended route (inner belt) will destroy or cripple constitute a primary scientific arsenal of democracy in this grueling struggle to maintain the balance of scientific power in the service of free men. The recommended line, for instance, definitely proposes to take the heart of the MIT Instrumentation Laboratory. It does so on the basis that if the laboratory is not actually taken, 'the vibrations from the adjacent freeway will hamper critically the usefulness of this laboratory.'

"What is going on in this Instrumentation Laboratory? In the areas to be taken, one thousand scientists, engineers, technicians and others are at mid-stride to develop guidance systems and components, including those for the Apollo mooncraft, and an advanced missile system for the Air Force called Sabre. This work may seem remote from your home and mine, but in reality it means a good deal to their ultimate safety.

"Thus throughout the world American submarines protect the frontiers of freedom with the Polaris missile. Where was the guidance system before Polaris developed? The answer is at the Instrumentation Laboratory of MIT. The efficiency of that single Polaris guidance system may actually be capable of saving from enemy attack more homes, more jobs, more businesses than would be lost through the location of one hundred inner-belt highways in the metropolitan areas of the East. Can the present and projected needs of MIT be ignored if, by disregarding them, we set back the development of the Apollo mooncraft for our astronauts in space, or an advanced missile system for the Air Force? Under these circumstances can the elected representatives of the City of Cambridge endorse any plan for the location of the inner-belt highway which is admittedly predicted on a study which clearly states (and again I quote), 'the effects of the alternate alignments of the present and projected needs of MIT were not a part of this study.' Those needs must be studied because they are the needs of Cambridge, the needs of Massachusetts, the needs of the nation and the needs of the free world—the needs of people and the needs of homes.

"Throughout Europe, the outlines of the great roads of ancient Rome are still visible, sad remnants of a civilization that has vanished, overrun by the tough invaders of its time. Will a traveler, centuries hence, trace the vestiges of the inner belt and sadly note that it was built at the cost of demolishing scientific facilities that might have effectively countered the blow that 'buried' us, to use Khrushchev's warning phrase?"

No radical student could have asked for a more convincing statement of the goals and functions of MIT. It is interesting that in his pleas Hanify never mentioned that MIT was educating anyone, and as a matter of fact, the labs that were to be affected don't involve faculty or students, but are run for the government.

In 1965 Harvard, MIT and a group of industrialists, notably Polaroid Corporation, established the Cambridge Corporation, a nonprofit community development corporation. They provided it with $1 million in funds, and brought in Oliver Brooks, brother of Harvey Brooks, the Harvard engineering dean, to run it. Cambridge Corporation is a publicity agent for the institutions and big companies in Cambridge, and also provides an intelligence network for them. Brooks tries to work with community groups, providing them with technical help in drawing up development plans, and so on. The results are skimpy: one tiny children's playground and a renovated two-story house. This feeble project was Polaroid's way of paying off the neighborhood for building parking lots in a residential area. Cambridge Corporation has its hands in plans for other neighborhoods, which allows it to control what goes on there, and also provides MIT and Harvard with intelligence on what is going to happen in these places.

Recently the Ford Foundation gave Harvard and MIT
$3 million each for urban studies; most of it was for en-
dowing chairs in the subject, and helped to increase the
budget of the Joint Center for Urban Studies. The
immediate result of this money was the hiring of Boston's
former Mayor John Collins as a professor. Daniel Moynihan is the director of the center, and it is understood that
he along with others in the Harvard School of Education
had initially pressed for action research programs, but
had failed to get them past Pusey. It's not entirely clear
what the function of the Joint Center is meant to be. It
has done long studies of the Colombian economy, and is
making an analysis of demands for health services in Boston. Moynihan himself was especially well known while in
the Department of Labor as a propagandizer for the Kennedy Administration. More recently he has seemed especially keen to collect data about social conditions.

At the press conference announcing the Ford grants,
Pusey, Moynihan and Howard Johnson, MIT's president,
set forth the Harvard-MIT line. Pusey declared, "It seems
to me that the significance of the Ford grant is a recognition that we just don't know enough yet about cities in
order to frame wise policies for correcting some of the
shortcomings that obviously exist in urban life. And the
whole nation is excited about this, has a new and heightened awareness of the need for action. Private individuals, foundations, city government, state government are
all going to be enacting programs, but the real deep understanding and wisdom for formation of policy just
doesn't exist, and what we're looking forward here toward is a research program that will begin to provide
some of the answers, or some of the knowledge and information . . ."

A black man spoke up, saying, "What will happen to
the city while you gentlemen are discussing what's supposed to be done? You have welfare rolls that are growing.
For instance, Harvard has a pretty good medical school.
Why couldn't they have a program to teach the welfare re-

cipients how to become nurses? There is a shortage of nurses. You could have your financial institutions put pressure on the banks to allow people to gain mortgages so they could build better housing. This type of thing should be going on while you're deciding what you're going to do with these people, or for these people. You're going to be studying them to death, I think."

"Well, sir," Moynihan said, "there's a great deal of activity like that going on at MIT and Harvard; more, no doubt, should, but I guess it's one of the dangers you have in the academic world, that is, forgetting that nobody elected you to anything, and quite seriously, I guess our first job is to sort out what we think we know or don't know about problems, and right at this moment we arc impressed by the number of things we don't know."

James Q. Wilson, former director of the center, added that perhaps in any ultimate sense, the answers may well be unknowable, but agitation of them to keep them before the public was well worth while.

"It's strange to sit here and hear you gentlemen say you don't know the answers," the black man said. "Now I think some of the solutions are very simple . . . All a man wants is a piece of bread, a halfway decent place to live and a job he can go to, to pay his bills, take care of his family, his kids to get a fair education. I think it is a simple problem."

Pusey said, "I quite like your statement about what a man wants, very, uh, very knowledgeable, and very meaningful to me. The question is how do we achieve those simple things. It's all a man wants, but it's not easy to achieve in areas where people are jammed together the way we are in cities all over the world. And we've got to learn more about the dynamics of that problem, and then train people to be able to deal with it. The statement of the problem is a relatively simple one, but the solution is a very complicated one."

A reporter asked why, instead of using the $6 million to establish chairs in urban studies, Harvard and MIT

had not turned the money, say, over to the people in
Roxbury, letting them set up some sort of community organization, through which they might develop their own
way of life and solve their own problems.

"Because the Ford Foundation gave it to us, I guess,"
Moynihan said, "because we can use it, and we're here.
And our activities—the function of universities is to study
and teach. It was given for that purpose and I think we're
happy to receive it for that purpose." He added, "We
should not like to suggest that we are anything but im-
mensely grateful to the Ford Foundation, but, sir, quite,
really, you know, would you say, you can rephrase your
question and ask why do you spend money on cancer research when you could give money to people who had
cancer? I mean, we are saying—and I think you would
miss the intellectual climate of these two universities at
this point—we are saying we don't think the answers to
these questions are adequately known, and we don't think
that until they are adequately known, you are going to be
able to do much about them, and that happens to be the
business of the universities, that and training people to
work in these things; that's our thing, and with this grant
we're going to do more of it."

Shortly after announcement of the Ford grants, a
neighborhood group in Roxbury met, and showing simple
good sense, voted to stay clear of any professor connected
with the Joint Center.

It would be difficult to find an institution of higher learning in the country so deeply and justly detested as is Columbia University in New York City. Even Julian Levi,
who has been there to shell out his advice, despairs of the
place.

Columbia dominates fifteen other institutions which
cling together along the upper West Side on Morningside
Heights, an area extending roughly from 110th to 125th
Street, and reaching from the Hudson River eastward up
on to Morningside Heights, which affords a commanding

view of the sprawling slums of Harlem. This is an area of three quarters of a square mile, holding 60,000 people, populated, in addition to Columbia, by, among others, Teachers College, Jewish Theological Seminary, Barnard, St. Luke's Hospital, Union Theological Seminary. Since World War II, Columbia and the others have slowly constructed a redoubt on the Heights, dislocating 7500 people, pushing out the poor, the Puerto Ricans and Negroes. Columbia is now working secretly and silently through its real estate subsidiaries, driving north deep into Harlem, east to Central Park, and to the south as far down as 96th Street. And even all this is not enough for the men who run this university. They speculate in land across the Hudson River in Rockland County, New York. All in all, while Columbia passes as a university, in reality it is among the great real estate development corporations of the time.

So that the educational institutions would not foul each other up by fighting for the same piece of land, they formed a united front in 1947 by creating Morningside Heights, Incorporated. This was David Rockefeller's idea. It works to coordinate plans of the different members but is clearly dominated by Columbia, which enters into deliberations or not as the occasion warrants it. Morningside Heights also serves as a publicity agent, operating several community programs meant to ingratiate the universities to the people of the neighborhood, and through Remedco, Incorporated, a real estate subsidiary, stands ready to form joint real estate syndications for the different institutions, purchase land and act as banker for schools that don't have the money on hand to buy the necessary land. Thus, when the Jewish Theological Semiry purchased land at the end of one block, and Columbia brought some at the other end, Morningside Heights got Columbia to exchange its land for some more land in another spot. Among its lesser contributions to community harmony is a Rotary Club, begun to bring together Harlem businessmen with members of the university community, especially the professors who are interested in studying the various facets of black life. And $100,000, or more than one-third of Morningside Heights' budget, is spent to employ a private guard and detective company to help protect residents of the Heights from thieves who steal up through Morningside Park and prey upon the faculty as they walk along the Drive. Morningside Heights, Incorporated, cooperates with the city police in staking out institution-owned buildings which are suspected of being narcotics drops.

So as not to discomfit the people it wants to evict from buildings the university buys, Columbia maintains a relocation office run by Ronald Golden. Golden says he relocates perhaps 200 people a year, many of them, elderly and white, who have been able to hang on in the Heights because they live in rent-controlled apartments. If there is one thing that infuriates every official at Columbia University it is the vulgar working-class persons who live in rent-controlled apartments and refuse to move. Golden relates bitterly the tale of an Irish bus driver and his wife who lived in a four-room apartment at $30 a month. They might have needed this large apartment with children growing up, but now they had no real use for it; but they were adamantly hanging on, saving enough money in the process to go to Ireland every summer. Golden says he could find for this couple and others like them similar apartments at $10 to $20 a month more on the edges of Harlem or further uptown around Puerto Rican neighborhoods, but these people don't care to go back near the ghettos, and so Golden had to track all over the city—out to Queens, up in the Bronx—looking for apartments. Golden says that his job, fortunately, is made somewhat easier because Columbia will pay a building manager a finder's fee to skip over his list of waiting applicants and sneak in their man.

Golden has little use for landlords either. He was especially disgusted by one group of landlords who on getting out of a German concentration camp came to the United

States and set themselves up in the real estate business. They bought a single-room-occupancy dwelling in the Columbia neighborhood for $250,000, then took the city for a ride. The mental hospitals were congested, and in an effort to ease this problem, New York was undertaking a pilot project whereby mental patients who looked as if they might make a go of it on the outside would be boarded out where they could get "home care." Since most of the patients were on welfare, and payment was assured, the landlords of the rooming house put in for home care. But there wasn't any home care. To protect himself, one building manager stationed himself within a wire mesh cage of the building, letting the patients and a mixture of pushers, pimps, lesbians, whores and hit men loose on the upper floors. Golden remembers that by the grace of God the inmates of this wretched dwelling were delivered from their new masters when Columbia bought the building in 1965 for $450,000. When Golden went along to see the new acquisition for himself, he remembers that the manager was afraid to go above the first floor for fear he would be stomped, and so were the police. This didn't bother Golden any. He applied the tried-and-true Columbia method, by offering each inmate $100 if he would leave the premises immediately. Most of them, never having seen so much money at one time before, gratefully accepted and fled.

In describing how Columbia got three families out of a building which they wanted to tear down to make way for a School of International Affairs, the *Spectator,* the student newspaper, said Golden "denied that Columbia had harassed the families in order to make them depart. Two weeks ago, however, the building's heating plant was demolished." As William Bloor, the university treasurer, described the policy: "When a tenant isn't behaving himself, we will move him out."

The Ford Foundation approached Columbia in the spring of 1967 to see whether it might not be interested in receiving a $10 million line of credit to run some

urban programs. According to President Kirk, he first
met with McGeorge Bundy of the Ford Foundation, and
this led to the creation of a five-man committee to organize the different projects.

The chairman was Clarence C. Walton, dean of the
School of General Studies, and while its members included representatives on the faculties of the law, journalism and business schools as well as Teachers College,
there were never any representatives from Harlem, or
from any of the Morningside Heights community groups.
Walton suspects this was so because it was not the purpose of the program to embrace people in the neighborhood. Rather, Ford was mainly interested in creating an
urban think tank. The motive concerned Columbia's internal politics as well, for the money was to entice the
more conservative sections of the university into taking
an interest in urban affairs. If this was the intention, then
it was a rather expensive way of getting rid of Jacques
Barzun, the book-club man and Columbia provost, who
about this time quit his job as provost and was replaced
by David Truman, a man alleged to represent progress.
Barzun was well known for his warm feelings toward the
surrounding community, which he referred to as "uninvit-
ing, abnormal, sinister, dangerous." He said that to move
about in the area, faculty and students had to display
"the perpetual qui vive of a paratrooper in enemy country."

In June, 1967, the Walton committee reported its findings and urged the creation of a Center on Urban-Minor-
ity Affairs, and after a long search for a suitable black
man, appointed Franklin H. Williams, U.S. ambassador
to Ghana, as the chairman. Ford handed over $2.8 mil-
lion as a first installment, and later on added some chairs
to attract learned gentlemen interested in studying urgent
matters affecting the cities—which usually means some
politician of Bundy's liking who was recently heisted out
of office.

The only Ford project that means anything to the

neighborhood is run by Mrs. Joan Shapiro of the community psychiatry division at St. Luke's Hospital. For several years Mrs. Shapiro has been trying to assist the people whom Columbia and the other institutions evict from the run-down rooming houses, or SRO's as they are more commonly called. Most of these people are unable to help themselves or to sustain any political action, and are therefore subject to the institutions' manipulations, but in the case of two buildings purchased by Columbia, Mrs. Shapiro's intervention resulted in the university's relocating the residents, not merely chucking them out on the street. In getting rid of these people, Columbia is contributing to a wholesale destruction of a way of life. Mrs. Shapiro's work is a mercy, but were the Ford Foundation really serious about this business, they would have provided her with the funds to buy several of the remaining SRO's, and work to preserve them, not rip them down.

The rest of Bundy's urban venture is trivial. Thirty-five law students spent the summer working for various city and neighborhood agencies, but according to Paul Dodyk, the professor in charge, the students do not work in Morningside Heights itself, and Mrs. Shapiro says that on many occasions when she needed help and called up the office, nobody answered the phone. The medical school is training six para-medical workers. Teachers College began with a swell idea for starting a community school, but now offers "expert" assistance to Harlem groups. Dr. Fritz Ianni, who manages this effort, says Teachers College spent much of its time dissociating itself from Columbia. Samuel Lubell, the pollster and professor at the Graduate School of Journalism, was a member of Walton's committee, which proposed to set up a special program to teach journalism students how to report "social change." Later on this was removed from the Ford urban program proper, and funded through some other channel at Ford. Intrigued by the various possibilities, I called up Lubell and asked him what they were doing. He said seven students were enrolled in the special program, which was an "effort to begin to learn how to report the process of change."

"When you say it involves new techniques of reporting change, what do you mean by this?" I asked.

"I don't know how to give it to you fast," Lubell said. "I could put together a press release and announcements of what we're doing."

"But can't you just tell me, basically, what the students do?"

"Well," said Lubell, "we're trying to get a better, . . . we're trying to develop, ah . . . it's a mixture of things we're trying to do. But we're trying to give them a better understanding of all these problems." Lubell said the students carried out individual studies. "We're combining the use of a whole lot of research data that have never been made available in this form to journalists."

"What kind of research data?"

"We're trying to measure how, uh . . . we're trying to figure change before it happens, and this involves trying to pull together all sorts of research data."

"But what specifically do you mean?"

"Now, our frame of focus is the whole racial problem. It's not the slums alone. We're interested in the slums. And we're trying to get a better analysis of the problem. The whole focus is on measuring and reporting change. The only reason I hesitate is that in outlining this program when it was first adopted, it took me an hour to explain it to the faculty, and I don't have a way of connecting with what you're after quickly. And I just don't have time to talk at random about this, I just don't know what you're after."

In June, 1967, the Office of Economic Opportunity made a one-year $400,000 demonstration grant through Columbia University to the Workshop for Development Planning, Harlem Commonwealth Council, to see whether a black group could begin its own business enterprises in Harlem when supplied with the expert technical advice of certain white organizations. The Commonwealth Council is run by Roy Innis, former Harlem CORE head. Under this plan, the Workshop for Development Planning was to carry out various economic studies in the area; the New School for Social Research would look into different kinds of small business. Donald Cook, the psychologist and expert in programmed instruction, was to figure out ways for training management. The Architects Renewal Committee for Harlem (ARCH) was to survey existing manufacturing and commercial facilities, and the research arm of the National Association of Manufacturers was to recommend the most efficient methods of operating different kinds of business.

Almost at once the OEO program ran into conflict with the Columbia Business School, which had initially received Ford money to implement its own odd idea for starting small businesses in Harlem. This program was drawn up under the direction of Hoke Simpson, associate dean of the Business School. He explained how the project began. Mayor Lindsay had established a special task force of business leaders to study the Harlem scene to see what might be done, but as is usual in such situations, everyone had forgotten about the group. But Simpson said the task force was very much in evidence, and indeed was about to issue a report suggesting, among other things, that Columbia University's Business School should establish an industrial development center in Harlem, a not altogether surprising proposition, since the school had prepared the studies on which the report was based. The center would be a storage bin for research on Harlem, provide experts to make marketing studies of the area, and in general serve as a broker to introduce Harlem and big business corporations to one another. This scheme swung on the school's own set of contacts in Harlem, which include Chase Manhattan's 135th Street office and the Freedom National Bank.

The difference between the Business School and OEO schemes created a quarrel among the faculty. Roy Innis threatened to produce screaming black hordes unless the

Business School's scheme was dropped. Finally it was squashed for the time being.

The main function of the Ford projects was to provide a publicity shield behind which the educational institutions on Morningside Heights, led by Columbia, continued their land grab. In 1965 Morningside Heights, Incorporated, presented the city with a map that indicated institutional expansion would halt on the south around 114th Street and Broadway, but two years later they had moved down to 110th Street, and at that point, announced expansion could be contained in a stretch running from 110th to 125th streets and from Riverside Drive along the Hudson River, east to the edge of Harlem on Morningside Drive. But after an official at Morningside Heights, Incorporated, described the area to me, he added, "We cannot solve our problems within these restricted boundaries." He went on to say that the institutions of higher learning needed a place to dump the residents of the buildings they took over. Eleven thousand more people are to be displaced in the next decade. And, indeed, he speculated that the newly awakened interest in studying Harlem, initiated by the Ford Foundation, might well result in creating a need for more buildings to house more professors who would be studying these urgent matters.

Columbia refuses to make public its real estate holdings. However, my inquiry, in the early part of 1968, indicated that Columbia has been quietly driving beyond its stated boundaries to the south. It picked up property on the south side of West 110th Street, taking up mortgages on West 101st Street and dickering through Morningside Heights for the purchase of the Paris Hotel on West 96th Street. To the east, the same official at Morningside Heights talked enthusiastically about the possibilities of redoing Douglas Circle, an entryway to Central Park. Meanwhile Columbia influenced the real estate market in another way. The university attached riders to leases for its apartment buildings, stating that should the tenants quit being students or leave the employ of the university, they then would have to give up the apartments, thus taking more housing off the rental market. The university continued to pay the building managers to take in people it was evicting ahead of others waiting in line. And despite Mrs. Shapiro's work, William Bloor continues to buy the remaining rooming houses, putting the people out. In one single-room-occupancy dwelling, inhabited by welfare clients and owned by the university on West 114th Street, the rent was increased 25 percent in December, 1967, with a threat of another increase for January. Charles F. Darlington, director of housing for Columbia, explained to the *Spectator* that the university raised rents "to encourage the few people who are still there to leave." Public pressure finally forced a postponement of the January increase. This rooming house was to be ripped down to make way for a new building to house the School of Social Work.

Meanwhile the university concluded its deal with the city for a lease to the southern section of Morningside Park, which lies as a sort of *cordon sanitaire* between itself and Harlem. Columbia leases the public park land for $3000 a year for 50 years, and until the siege of last spring, was planning to construct an unusual gymnasium there, complete with duplicate facilities—one set with a door opening on the Heights for the university athletes; the other, with a back door opening on the park into Harlem. Originally this was the price Columbia was made to pay for use of the land, but after the siege the plans were put into abeyance. In the fall of 1968 Kirk resigned as president, and all university policy was in limbo.

In carrying forward its real estate program, Columbia enjoys a cordial relationship with Percy Uris, chairman of the board of Uris Buildings Corporation, a large realty company. In the office of the president of Columbia University, Uris is listed as "special advisor to the president for new construction." He is also a Columbia trustee and chairman of the Finance Committee that oversees the university's investments, which include 33,422 shares of Uris Buildings common stock. Uris Buildings Corporation leases from Columbia a valuable piece of land at the foot of Wall Street. Uris got a $22.5 million construction loan for the Wall Street building from Irving Trust Company, where William E. Peterson is the president. In 1966 when the lease was negotiated, Peterson was a Columbia trustee and in 1967 he was made head of the trustees. The new Uris building is leased by the First National City Bank, where Allen H. Temple, another Columbia trustee, is former vice-chairman. As an indication of how careful the university is when it comes to even the remotest suspicion of conflict of interest, a trustee told me how this deal was brought off. When it came time for the trustees to vote on the deal, Uris left the room. Adrian Massie, another Columbia trustee, who also sits on the board of Uris Buildings, did not vote. Neither did Benjamin Buttenwieser, who is also a Columbia trustee and is financial consultant to Uris Buildings Corporation. My informant said they actually managed to get a quorum of thirteen trustees— who had nothing whatever to do with Uris—to approve the deal.

One of the Uris Buildings' main projects is at Blue Hill in Orangetown in Rockland County, thirty miles outside of New York on the west side of the Hudson River. Here Uris plans to build a complex of office and research buildings, easily accessible to New York City. This is not far from where Columbia maintains laboratories, and oddly enough, within a few minutes' drive from where the university took out an option to buy 545 acres, also in Orangetown, where Columbia is thinking about building 1000 homes for the faculty.

Another director of Uris Buildings Corporation is Courtney Brown, the dean of Columbia's Graduate School of Business. Together with his wife, Brown holds 1566 shares in Uris common stock. His office is in a gaudy modern aluminum-trimmed structure called, after the contributor who made its construction possible, the Uris Building.

A former economist with Standard Oil of New Jersey, Brown is a director and on the executive committees of Associated Dry Goods Corporation, American Electric Power Company and Union Pacific Railroad, where, as luck would have it, sits another Columbia trustee—emeritus—Walter D. Fletcher. Recently Brown was added to the board of directors of CBS, whose chairman, William Paley, is another Columbia trustee. All in all, at this writing in the spring of 1968, Brown held $168,000 in stock in these companies alone. These various relationships allow Brown to act as a sort of small-time broker for various interest groupings.

Brown handled the negotiations for Columbia in working up the so-called Piers area development plan, a grandiose scheme concocted by Columbia to house faculty (and dump the people it wants to get out of the Heights). The Piers area is a rundown strip of factories and warehouses between 125th and 135th streets, from Broadway to the river. It is relatively inexpensive land by New York standards, and for this reason, is a political football. Joe Overton, executive secretary of the Negro Labor Committee, has long laid claim to the Piers waterfront, over which he wanted to construct some sort of garden apartments. But according to one theory, the mud was deep, and it would be costly to put up the pilings on which the thing could be built.

Meanwhile Columbia was looking for a place to house the people it wanted out of the Heights, and it needed faculty housing. Moreover, some of the Columbia faculty were embarrassed about the Defense laboratories on the campus, and smitten as well with the idea of building an enclave for science-based industry along the Stanford model. In the fall of 1967 the electronics laboratory which works on ballistic missiles for the Defense Department was spun off from Columbia and became Riverside Research Institute. Its president, Lawrence O'Neill, went on leave as a professor at Columbia. Grayson Kirk, along with other officials from New York universities, sat on the institute's board of directors, and it is O'Neill's hope that the institute will be a place where professors from several schools can bring their work. One of O'Neill's ideas is to start a training institute that can take on people from Harlem and teach them how to become computer technicians, work in sub-professional jobs that are opening up in medicine, and so forth. He wants Riverside Research to get very much involved in medical electronics.

By late 1967, Columbia jumped the 125th Street boundary and began buying land in the Piers area. It purchased or held mortgages on properties running from 125th to 130th street. A trustee told me it was the university's intention to buy as much of the area as it could lay its hands on. Brown was sent along to work an arrangement with Joe Overton. At this stage of the game, it would have been crude to go into Harlem without some kind of black front. Since Overton's group existed as little more than a letterhead, it was perfect cover. Moreover, to clinch the deal the university needed some city-owned repair shops in the area, and required state aid to construct the building. Brown arranged a compromise with Overton. While the plans shifted back and forth, the basic idea was to construct a housing project atop a platform erected over the area. Underneath the platform there would be factories, garages and a supermarket which would hopefully employ people from Harlem. However, plans for the industrial area suggested it would be dominated by science-based businesses which require high-level skills. On top of the platform Overton could build apartments overlooking the water and with easy access to a park and a marina. Overton would handle the financing of the apartments, one third of which would be held for Columbia faculty. The others would be for people in Harlem, as well as those displaced by institutional expansion in Morningside Heights. The bulk of the apartments would be middle to upper income. Columbia would finance the construction of the industrial area, presumably through a pool of insurance companies. A figure of $200 million was mentioned as the cost.

"Who would construct this project?" asked an inquiring student.

"I have the agreement of the best builder in town to build it without profit," Brown said.

"Who would that be?" asked the student.

"Percy Uris," replied Brown.

When part of the above material was published last spring, first in a magazine article and then taken up by *The New York Times,* Uris declared, "I as an individual have told Courtney Brown that I would devote myself to this project without compensation or reward." In October, 1968, Columbia claimed to have reduced its role in the Piers project to that of consultant.

And thus Columbia went about building its redoubt. By throwing the poor Negroes and Puerto Ricans out of the single-room-occupancy dwellings, it reduces the number of poor minority types in the neighborhood, pressuring most of them into a smaller and smaller area of rundown dreadful rooming houses, now situated along West 85th Street. There are 30,000 of these transients—sick, desperate, dying people—on the West Side of New York. The poor whites of Columbia's own faculty from less prosperous days are deposited on the edges of Queens or the Bronx.

While the university engages in those odd Ford Foundation social programs, it refuses to educate the people in its own community. Of 2700 undergraduates, only 100 are black. Whereas ten years ago Columbia might at least claim to be a city university in the sense that nearly 60 percent of the students came from New York, now only 23 percent are from the city. Like the University of Chicago, Columbia pursues the fantasy of imitating Harvard, making the leap backward from a twenty-fifth-rate Ivy League school in 1968 to a nineteenth-century academy of excellence, an illusion which can only be brought about by constructing an armed camp with public funds.

Even after the students took control of part of the university and later went on to work with the community people in seizing an apartment building owned by Columbia on Morningside Heights, there was little indication that the university seriously intended to alter its basic structure so as to allow some change for the better. The investigatory commission of outsiders headed by Archibald Cox looked like a feeble public relations gesture. As for those dilettantes, the "concerned" professors who held hands as a symbol of defiance before the police broke into the student-held buildings, there is no reason to expect anything from them but long strings of articles in learned journals. The professors at Columbia don't know who runs their factory, or how it is run. They don't especially care. What they care about in the end is preserving their jobs.

Across New York City in Brooklyn, Long Island University, the tenth largest private insititution of higher learning in the nation, uses the lower classes in a rather more enterprising way. Whereas Columbia mounts a land grab under the guise of a social-uplift scheme, LIU collects enrollment fees from 8000 lower-middle-class students on their Brooklyn campus, packs them into an old movie house which has been redone into classrooms, and then siphons off $1 million or more a year to invest in fancy realty ventures out in the plush sections of Long Island. This business had been going on for some time, but it broke into the open early in 1967 when William M. Birenbaum, provost at the university's Brooklyn Center was forced to resign by R. Gordon Hoxie, the chancellor of the university.

Part of the dispute between the two men involved a difference in educational philosophy. Hoxie, a professional educator, is proud of having had a hand in building up LIU from a school with 1800 students a decade ago to what is now one of the largest universities in the country. LIU has 18,000 students on three different campuses—at Brooklyn, Westbury and Southampton—with plans to build law schools, MIT-like engineering complexes, oceanographic institutes, and so on, until it is in fact another sprawling multiversity.

On the other hand, Birenbaum, who had come to the Brooklyn Center two years before from the New School for Social Research in Manhattan, worked hard to involve the center with the adjacent Fort Greene slums. He wanted to improve academic standards; and perhaps most important, he wanted to reduce tuition from the then $1580 a year, not raise it to $1676 as Hoxie had ordered for 1967.

A few months before Birenbaum was fired, a small group of people from the Brooklyn campus met privately with Mrs. Mary Lai, the university's treasurer. She told them that the Brooklyn Center showed a surplus of about $1 million a year for each of the previous three years. But when Birenbaum then asked if that money could not be used to hold down tuition costs, Mrs. Lai replied that it was impossible because the excess funds were only a "paper surplus."

This led to charges by the Brooklyn faculty and students that the money for their campus had, in fact, been siphoned off to finance other university projects, some of them known, some unknown. And this in turn fed the students' suspicions that the members of the board of trustees might be using the university to advance their own business interests. They were furious at Birenbaum's firing and struck the Brooklyn Center. The accusations were vague, but nonetheless were the same kind of charges heard increasingly on other college campuses, and so I made an effort to look into this aspect of the LIU matter.

The university's board of trustees meets in private, and as is the case in many other private institutions, is self-perpetuating. LIU refuses to make public any sort of detailed financial report; nor will it show an investment portfolio. So, in fact, it exists as a tax-exempt secret organization.

Of the twenty-three members of the trustees' board, three were generally acknowledged to swing some real power. William Zeckendorf, Sr., the real estate man, was chairman of the board, and his son, William Zeckendorf, Jr., was a trustee as well. The elder Zeckendorf became a member of the board in 1942 when LIU was in deep financial trouble, and he helped it along with both advice and money. The Brooklyn campus is named after him, and even those among the faculty and students who are critical of the trustees seemed fond of Zeckendorf and credited him with helping the university make a go of it. Arthur T. Roth, a Republican and chairman of the Franklin National Bank, did much to build up banking on Long Island, and Franklin National is an enormous enterprise which played a large part in the development of Long Island. Roth did business with Zeckendorf, and was a director of Webb & Knapp when Zeckendorf ran it. Webb & Knapp owed Franklin National $1.3 million when it went into bankruptcy in 1965. (Another LIU trustee, General James Van Fleet, was also a director of Webb & Knapp during Zeckendorf's reign there.)

In 1964 Zeckendorf gave LIU a tract of land near Brookhaven Laboratory at Yaphank to be used as an engineering center. This was meant to be an attractive site for Long Island University, since it was across the road from a major atomic research center, and, presumably, the idea was that the two institutions would somehow relate to each other. This would have worked out well from the point of view of Webb & Knapp, which at the time was interested in developing the Yaphank property into a development for science-based industry, and from all accounts the scheme looked a little like an imitation of the University of California's Irvine campus, with LIU providing a packaged community to live in Zeckendorf's reality development. As it turned out, this plan caved in because Webb & Knapp went bankrupt, and while LIU pushed on with its plans for an engineering center, it has not yet started one.

In an interview, Hoxie said Franklin National had loaned the university money from time to time and helped out with mortgages, all on very advantageous terms to LIU. Hoxie maintained that the university did business with banks other than those run by university trustees. However, I later found out that the university's main account had been shifted from the Chemical Bank New York Trust Company to Franklin National shortly after Hoxie was made chancellor in 1964. This is an important piece of business, since LIU has a $30 million annual budget. In 1967 Franklin National gave LIU $100,000 to help it set up a consortium of universities, which LIU hoped could buy land on Montauk Point, at the end of Long Island, and there set up an oceanographic institute. This would be an interesting scientific endeavor, especially since LIU is not well known for its studies in oceanography, but it would benefit Montauk Point. The economy there booms in the summer with the tourist trade, but business is dead in the winter. An oceanographic institute, employing middle-class technocrats, would operate the year around, and provide a small basic industry for the Point. This is all very much in Franklin National's interest, since it holds mortgages on much of the land surrounding the site of the project. The question in both this case and that of the engineering facility was really whether LIU ought to engage in such elaborate plans at the same time that its faculty was complaining about poor academic standards. Its political and economic development seemed almost directly opposite to its efforts to improve teaching.

The vice-chairman and secretary of the board was John P. McGrath, an old-line Democrat who had been a corporation counsel under Mayor William O'Dwyer in the late 1940's. McGrath became a trustee during that time; he is now chairman of East New York Savings Bank and involved in developing real estate, and since the fall of 1967, has been chairman of the university's trustees. According to Hoxie, McGrath's bank has been generous in lending the university money and holding mortgages on its properties at reduced rates. (In fact, East New York Savings holds mortgages on the Southampton campus.) McGrath's brother, Francis, is assistant secretary to the board of trustees, but he doesn't have a vote. He also is the university's counsel and gets a retainer of $15,000 a year. In recent years several other tired Democratic politicians have attached themselves to LIU. Former New York Mayor Robert Wagner is on the executive council at Southampton College, LIU's branch at the far end of the island. Hoxie appointed Edward Cavanagh, Wagner's brother-in-law and former New York City Fire Commissioner, to be chairman of the Development Council for C.W. Post College—the mid-island campus of LIU. James J. Wilson, who was an education consultant to Wagner when he was mayor, is the university's director of development. Paul R. Screvane, the former deputy mayor in Wagner's time, is vice-president of MacCleans Service Company, Incorporated, the company the university hires to clean up on the three campuses. MacCleans got the contract at the Brooklyn Center a couple of years ago, and it is substantial, amounting to $180,000 a year for that center alone.

While it might have been possible to separate these different interests by looking through financial reports, or records of trustee meetings which might provide some clue as to how decisions were made, LIU has refused to make them public.

The protests against Birenbaum's sacking gradually wore down, and the student-faculty coalition which had struck and closed the Brooklyn Center disintegrated. The professors, fearful of losing their jobs, crossed the picket lines. (Students always seem to make the mistake in these events of striking alliances with professors, whose interests run opposite to theirs.) As is often the case in these protests, a committee of professors was appointed to work privately with the trustees to try to iron out the complaints. But this was not taken seriously, and to all intents and purposes the strike was over.

Meanwhile Hoxie urged the people at the Brooklyn Center to quit fighting over matters of internal administration, and get about the business of making Long Island University a truly great institution. The blueprint for the future was set forth in a ten-year plan, which called for beginning a new law school, an engineering complex and a graduate school of social work to be headquartered at the Brooklyn Center; a major medical complex, a health sciences center, and so on. All this was disclosed in February, 1967, a little before the Birenbaum dismissal, and at that time Hoxie was quoted in *The New York Times* as saying, "It is a bold and imaginative plan—certainly as exciting as *The Perils of Pauline*—to help keep the private universities in the forefront despite the overwhelming support for public education." Hoxie evidently had no intention of being overwhelmed by the expanding state and city university systems, for in August of that year he wrote the faculty, promising them that unlike the University of Buffalo, which had given in and joined the public State University of New York system, LIU would not be dismembered.

Hardly had the professors received this notice, than it was announced in the newspapers that Long Island University was selling the Brooklyn Center to the City University of New York, which wanted to turn it into a new business school. LIU claimed it reached the decision to sell after consulting with Dr. Henry Heald, the former president of the Ford Foundation, who had been making a study of the university's operations, which it refused to make public. Hoxie said the Brooklyn Center was losing money and constituted a drag on the rest of the LIU system. And he promised the students and professors at Brooklyn that they could come to work or study at the Post campus, about fifty miles away from Brooklyn, or at the Southampton campus, 100 miles outside the city. This plan was impractical for the students, who would be hard put to pay for the transportation back and forth.

At this point a group made up of faculty and alumni decided to fight Hoxie and the trustees; they hired a public relations firm specializing in political ventures, and entered the Congolese politics of New York. Joseph Kottler, a liberal Democrat who heads an education committee in the state legislature, was interested in the situation, and he agreed to hold hearings on the proposed sale. Kottler repeatedly asked Hoxie and John McGrath, who by this time had been made chairman of the board of trustees, for the university's books and records, but his request was refused. Hoxie, rather, continued to quote figures that showed the Brooklyn Center was running a deficit. But Kottler's committee finally got its hands on a financial statement that had been given to the trustees; and it showed just the opposite: the Brooklyn Center was running an annual surplus of $1.7 million, while the campus at Westbury was in the hole $230,000 and the one at Southampton ran a deficit of $1.2 million.

None of the university representatives could remember precisely how they had arrived at the selling price of $32 million for the Brooklyn Center. They did admit no appraisal had been made. But they said that once the debts on the Brooklyn property were cleared, LIU should have $15 million in profit to apply to clearing the debts at the other campuses, and for starting up some of Hoxie's other projects, such as the law school and engineering complex.

On closely examining the LIU controller, the committee discovered that the university was able to show that the Brooklyn Center was in debt by arbitrarily changing the fiscal year from twelve to fifteen months (this was accomplished by including the summer, when there was no income). Thus, by comparing a twelve-month period against a fifteen-month period, the center showed a deficit.

When Hoxie was confronted with the blueprint of the

ten-year plan, which he had signed and for which he had written a preface, he denied having any part of it, and claimed the whole thing was the work of the Brooklyn Center people, who had put over a hoax on him. Kottler sought to discover when Hoxie first entertained the idea of selling the Brooklyn Center to the City University, but Hoxie's memory failed him. However, after considerable prodding he was able to recall discussions during the spring of 1967, and one on August 28, two days before he wrote the faculty that LIU would not be dismembered if he could help it, and just before he permitted the enrollment of 2000 freshmen who came on the assumption that they were taking up a four-year course of study at the Brooklyn Center. It was subsequently disclosed that shortly after the students began the semester, LIU quietly suspended all future admissions, which assured that if the Brooklyn Center did not then have a deficit, it soon would.

Late in the spring of 1967, Mayor Lindsay came out against the sale of LIU's Brooklyn Center to the City University, so that deal was squashed. But it still remained uncertain whether LIU would continue to run the place or try to palm it off on another buyer. Hoxie resigned as chancellor during autumn, 1968.

The virtue of LIU's Brooklyn Center was that it had really begun to assume the extremely difficult stance of educating poor youngsters without the usual prerequisites, and that it was moving into the slums, not with social uplift schemes, but with educational programs. But then, as McGrath explained to the *New York Post,* LIU was not in business "to deal with children who can't pay tuition."

9. Conclusion

The idea that the university is a community of scholars is a myth. The professors are less interested in teaching students than in yanking the levers of their new combines so that these machines will grow bigger and go faster. The university has in large part been reduced to serving as banker-broker for the professors' outside interests. The charming elitism of the professors has long since given way to the greed of the social and political scientists whose manipulative theories aim only at political power. Meanwhile the undergraduate students lie in campus holding pens, while graduate apprentices read them stories. The stories are boring, and students turn to making their own "free universities" or spend their time hatching political revolutions on the outside.

There are certain structural changes of a democratic bent that might assist universities in regaining the interest of their professors and students in education, and if some of these were taken up, then at least it would be possible to advantageously discuss the politics of these institutions.

The principle that should govern higher education, and all education in America, surely is simple enough: Since educational institutions are generally regarded as serving a public function, and financed to a large extent by the general citizenry, they ought to be responsible to the public. The different institutions should be run by students, teachers and administrators who are concerned with education. And they should be free to all.

193

This would require some changes in the manner in which these institutions now function. For one thing, no college or university whose members of its governing board are self-perpetuating should be eligible for public funding. Because of the present method of governing institutions of higher learning, there is an opportunity for a small group of men to use a university for their own ends. Since these institutions bear public responsibilities and receive much of their money from government they should be made responsible to the public and trustees should be elected—for terms of perhaps four to six years—by the students, alumni, faculty and other members of the immediate university community.

Trustees should not be selected because their private business interests may be useful to the college, but rather because of their views toward education. One way to move in this direction would be to prohibit members of the board of trustees from transacting any business with the university. Business dealings should be made at arm's length, and not by members of some club. To make it possible for younger people and poor people to become university trustees, there might well be a stipend for this work, and the trustees should have an expert staff so that, in fact, they can understand and intelligently criticize the work of the administration.

Meetings of the governing boards of a university should be public. So should the meetings of other groups whose decisions bear on the conduct of the university (i.e., faculty and student meetings). A reporter should be present during all of these gatherings, to make verbatim records, which can then be transcribed and published. In dealing with especially delicate matters, which would entail the trustees' holding executive sessions, the transcript of these sessions should receive timely publication. Disclosure is one way to protect the public's interests. If this sort of procedure had been in practice during Columbia's negotiations for the cigarette-filter patent, or during its land grab on 125th Street, there at least would have been a chance to alert people to what was going on. Surely these modest provisions should be in effect before any public official takes on the role of trustee in a private university. Among the trustees at Columbia is Frank Hogan, the district attorney of the City of New York, who in the case of the Piers renewal project placed himself in the position of being party to a real estate deal pending before New York City in behalf of a private corporation. He has no business being involved in such deals. Neither does Frederick Van Pelt Bryan, a federal district judge, who is also a trustee of Columbia University.

Moreover, the federal government should require all universities to issue publicly each quarter a detailed financial report, including an investment portfolio, showing any and all changes in holdings of securities, real estate and other types of investments. Each year the trustees and officers of universities should be required to furnish additional public statements that show their business affiliations, stock and property holdings. Harvard University's relations with the State Street Investment Corporation ought to be broken off, and so should all others like it. The Congress should block investment companies from profiting by combining their assets with those of tax-exempt educational institutions in seeking market leverage. Educational institutions are not meant to control industrial organizations. Yale University does not receive public funds to enhance its position as an educational institution so that it might better promote a mutual fund; its investment company should be disbanded. In general, McGeorge Bundy's proposal that the universities play the stocks more shrewdly is not wise, for the result is merely to involve them more intimately in the market, which in turn makes them more dependent on the profits of large companies and less inclined to criticize their activities.

University administrators, in particular their presidents, should be directed to run the affairs of the university; they are paid well to do so. They should be prohibited from sitting on the boards of directors of any company, foundation, government agency, or any other group. As Kingman Brewster observed, these relationships are more apt to raise competing interests and are a waste of time.

Professors are paid by the university to teach students, not to lobby. If they want to work for the CIA or some soap company, then they should quit and do so. If they enter into consulting arrangements with government or business, these should be disclosed, along with the fee, if one is paid.

As for professors who have articles published in university publications, law journals and reviews, Justice William O. Douglas suggests, "I propose an editorial policy that puts in footnote number one the relevant affiliations of the author. If the article is paid for, I would not necessarily require the disclosure of the amount of the fee; the fact that there was a fee would be sufficient. If there is no fee, but a client's interest was reflected in the article, I would want disclosure of that client's identity. If the author was a free-lancer in a particular field, I would want a general statement that his professional interest lay in the direction of certain types of litigation."

While the members of the Congress may consider it a matter of amusement that this or that professor appears before them without disclosing that he has in fact been retained by some company or other interested party, this should not be taken lightly. The testimony is often printed and distributed around the country and may well mislead public opinion. It should be made doubly clear to witnesses before the Congress that they must disclose any connection with the matter at hand.

The undergraduate students, who now have little or no say in how the university should be run, would, as suggested above, be included in the community that selects the governors. They might also insist on granting bodies of student government the veto power over major university decisions, such as admissions and finances. The typical argument against giving students a voice in running a university is that they are transient and young. In fact, they

are no more transient than a member of the House of
Representatives, who serves a two-year term. As for their
youth, it was the students, not the faculty or administrators, who raised and kept after the war research issue.
What is unusual about the student revolts is that the undergraduates have displayed so much interest in attempting to get the universities back to teaching. When one
considers that all they got for their trouble was the creation, one after the other, of deadly independent investigatory commissions controlled by the faculty proprietors
and headed by labor mediators, their patience and good
sense seem extraordinary.

Prying open the universities by changing around their
organizational framework does not necessarily mean that
their politics will also change. It is often dimly understood by the administrators of these places that the radicals who demand more of a say for the students are not
representative of the great mass of undergraduates, many
of whom are conservative. Nonetheless, at the very least a
change in structure opens the possibility of influencing the
shape of the policies through a democratic process, and
the students will be a little better off for knowing a bit
more about the operations of the institutions.

One may hope that the country will pursue the idea
that a university is a place where great teachers and students are brought together. It doesn't really matter
whether this occurs on the campus of some quaint Ivy
League college or in the streets of Harlem, and surely the
impedimenta which are used by the faculty guilds to stifle
decent teachers ought to be done away with. What difference does it make whether the instructor has a degree, or
how many books and honors he has to his name? It really
is not especially important whether the student comes
along for two or four or six years, or whether he gets a
diploma, or for that matter whether he meets the en-
trance standards some psychologist has laid out for him to
meet. One of the most useful endeavors in higher education would be to get rid of the bachelor's degree entirely,

thereby doing away with a false admissions slip into the upper middle classes, and into the dreary academic guilds.

Secret research, whether it is performed as proprietary work for a company or the government, has no place in a university. It stands between the institution and a free society. This is not to say that the universities should not undertake controversial projects. People might now be alive had Cornell used its information about cars to challenge large corporations, rather than lying down meekly before the automobile makers and taking their money in exchange for silence.

In the case of the large city universities, it may well prove useful for the residents of the neighborhoods in which they exist to view these institutions for what they are, sort of de facto governments; and in exchange for suffering their presence, wring some concessions. The deals will differ depending on the locale. But it may make good sense for the residents of Hyde Park in Chicago or Morningside Heights in New York to insist on electing the presidents, respectively, of the University of Chicago and Columbia. They may also want guarantees of certain unskilled jobs, including those in the social science research projects, and receive free college education for their children. In the case of the University of Chicago, Columbia, Harvard or MIT, this would mean that the professors would find it necessary to spend a certain amount of their time in the streets teaching ignorant people. But this wouldn't hurt them. In recent years the clergy has found it a bracing experience to rediscover the parish, and the teacher may find it equally refreshing to meet some students.

Appendix

DEFENSE CONTRACTORS

NON-PROFIT INSTITUTIONS—Fiscal Year 1967

RANK	NAME OF CONTRACTOR AND LOCATION		THOUSANDS OF DOLLARS
14 Massachusetts Institute of Technology			92,423*
Washington	D.C.		75
Bedford	Massachusetts		170
Boston	Massachusetts		200
Cambridge	Massachusetts		48,238
Lexington	Massachusetts		43,740
22 Johns Hopkins University			71,041*
Washington	D.C.		42
Baltimore	Maryland		3,299
Silver Spring	Maryland		67,700
23 Aerospace Inc.			70,827*
El Segundo	California		70,616
San Bernardino	California		211
31 Stanford Research Institute			30,617*
	Iran		99
	Thailand		500
Huntsville	Alabama		37
Menlo Park	California		29,798
Stanford	California		68
Las Vegas	Nevada		115
39 Mitre Corp.			20,942*
Bedford	Massachusetts		20,942
42 Rand Corporation			19,322*
Santa Monica	California		19,322

DEFENSE CONTRACTORS

NON-PROFIT INSTITUTIONS—Fiscal Year 1967 *(Cont'd.)*

RANK	NAME OF CONTRACTOR AND LOCATION		THOUSANDS OF DOLLARS
43	System Development Corporation		19,078*
	Lompoc	California	350
	Los Angeles	California	25
	Santa Monica	California	17,294
	Belleville	Illinois	404
	Rome	New York	240
	Dayton	Ohio	260
	Falls Church	Virginia	483
	Norfolk	Virginia	22
45	California University of		17,353*
	Berkeley	California	8,050
	Davis	California	181
	Irvine	California	62
	La Jolla	California	2,403
	Los Angeles	California	1,803
	Riverside	California	101
	San Diego	California	3,287
	San Francisco	California	368
	Santa Barbara	California	954
	Sepulveda	California	24
	Holloman AFB	New Mexico	20
46	Cornell Aeronautical Laboratory Inc.		17,111*
	Edwards	California	83
	Buffalo	New York	16,678
	Falls Church	Virginia	358
48	Columbia University		16,416*
		Foreign	34
	Point Arena	California	90
	New York	New York	15,782
	Palisades	New York	510
49	Institute for Defense Analysis		15,823*
	Washington	D.C.	3,389
	Arlington	Virginia	12,434
53	Stanford University		14,875*
	Pacific Grove	California	20
	Palo Alto	California	4,470
	Stanford	California	10,385

DEFENSE CONTRACTORS

NON-PROFIT INSTITUTIONS—Fiscal Year 1967 (*Cont'd.*)

RANK	NAME OF CONTRACTOR AND LOCATION		THOUSANDS OF DOLLARS
58 Michigan, University of			13,714*
		Thailand	300
	Honolulu City	Hawaii	1,260
	Ann Arbor	Michigan	11,526
	Willow Run	Michigan	349
	Ypsilanti	Michigan	279
59 I I T Research Institute			13,517*
	Chicago	Illinois	8,986
	Elwood	Illinois	15
	Annapolis	Maryland	4,496
	Wright Patters	Ohio	20
60 Research Analysis Corporation			13,289*
		Iran	745
		Vietnam	53
	McLean	Virginia	11,649
	Varicus	Domestic	842
67 Franklin Institute of Pennsylvania			11,293*
	Philadelphia	Pennsylvania	11,275
	Swarthmore	Pennsylvania	18
69 Illinois University of			10,961*
	Urbana	Illinois	4,955
	Chicago	Illinois	322
	Urbana	Illinois	5,684
71 Pennsylvania State University			9,808*
	University Park	Pennsylvania	9,808
80 Battelle Memorial Institute			6,804*
	Lompoc	California	328
	Columbus	Ohio	6,210
	Richland	Washington	266
81 Cornell University			6,713*
	Arecibo	Puerto Rico	1,800
	Ithaca	New York	4,776
	New York	New York	137
89 United States Natl Aero Space Agency			6,070*
		Netherlands	18

DEFENSE CONTRACTORS

NON-PROFIT INSTITUTIONS—Fiscal Year 1967 (*Cont'd.*)

RANK	NAME OF CONTRACTOR AND LOCATION		THOUSANDS OF DOLLARS
	Sacramento	California	11—
	Washington	D.C.	164
	St. Louis	Missouri	1,984—
	Ridgeley	W. Virginia	7,883
96	Washington, University of		5,618
	Seattle	Washington	5,618
101	Woods Hole Oceanographic Institute		5,158*
	Woods Hole	Massachusetts	5,158
106	Pennsylvania University of		4,833*
	Urbana	Illinois	59
	Philadelphia	Pennsylvania	4,774
107	Princeton University		4,831*
	Princeton	New Jersey	4,831
109	Texas University of		4,618*
	Washington	D.C.	50
	Alamogordo	New Mexico	37
	White Sands MS	New Mexico	40
	Austin	Texas	3,964
	Dallas	Texas	19
	El Paso	Texas	228
	Galveston	Texas	228
	Houston	Texas	52
111	George Washington University		4,534*
	Washington	D.C.	4,534
116	Harvard University		4,247*
	Boston	Massachusetts	507
	Cambridge	Massachusetts	2,751
	Fort Davis	Texas	160
	Cambridge	Massachusetts	829
117	California Institute of Technology		4,189*
	Pasadena	California	4,189
119	Ohio State University Research Foundation		4,137*
	Columbus	Ohio	3,842
	Dayton	Ohio	14
	Wright Patters	Ohio	281

DEFENSE CONTRACTORS

NON-PROFIT INSTITUTIONS—Fiscal Year 1967 (Cont'd.)

RANK	NAME OF CONTRACTOR AND LOCATION		THOUSANDS OF DOLLARS
120	Southwest Research Institute		4,124*
	Wright Patters	Ohio	417
	San Antonio	Texas	3,707
125	Dayton, University of		3,860*
	Dayton	Ohio	3,646
	Wright Patters	Ohio	214
131	Duke University		3,380*
	Durham	North Carolina	3,380
133	Denver, University of		3,271*
	Denver	Colorado	3,271
140	Miami, University of		2,879*
	Coral Gables	Florida	1,268
	Miami	Florida	1,611
141	National Academy of Sciences		2,849*
	Washington	D.C.	2,849
143	Carnegie Institute of Technology		2,836*
	Pittsburgh	Pennsylvania	2,836
144	New Mexico State University		2,811*
	Alamogordo	New Mexico	28
	Las Cruces	New Mexico	386
	University Park	New Mexico	2,397
147	Syracuse University Research Corporation		2,716*
	Syracuse	New York	2,716
150	American University		2,668*
		UAR	14
	Washington	D.C.	2,654
152	Maryland, University of		2,565*
	Washington	D.C.	24
	Baltimore	Maryland	1,343
	College Park	Maryland	1,198
154	New York University		2,500*
	Bronx	New York	539
	Washington Square	New York	1,961

DEFENSE CONTRACTORS

NON-PROFIT INSTITUTIONS—Fiscal Year 1967 (*Cont'd.*)

RANK	NAME OF CONTRACTOR AND LOCATION		THOUSANDS OF DOLLARS
155	Chicago, University of		2,393*
	Chicago	Illinois	2,393
165	Purdue Research Foundation		2,218*
	Lafayette	Indiana	2,180
	West Lafayette	Indiana	38
169	Brown University		2,146*
	Providence	Rhode Island	2,146
173	Northwestern University		2,114*
	Evanston	Illinois	2,114
176	Utah, University of		2,066*
	Dugway	Utah	334
	Salt Lake City	Utah	1,743
177	Colorado University		2,066*
	Boulder	Colorado	1,740
	Denver	Colorado	326
179	Brooklyn Polytechnic Institute		2,035*
	Brooklyn	New York	1,877
	Farmingdale	New York	158
180	Midwest Research Institute		2,325*
	Kansas City	Missouri	1,810
	Wright Patters	Ohio	225
186	Wisconsin, University of		1,953*
	Madison	Wisconsin	1,953
189	Minnesota, University of		1,915*
	Minneapolis	Minnesota	1,915
193	New York, State University of		1,823*
	Albany	New York	272
	Brooklyn	New York	273
	Buffalo	New York	348
	New York	New York	799
	Stony Brook	New York	100
	Syracuse	New York	31

DEFENSE CONTRACTORS

NON-PROFIT INSTITUTIONS—Fiscal Year 1967 (Cont'd.)

RANK	NAME OF CONTRACTOR AND LOCATION		THOUSANDS OF DOLLARS
197	Pittsburgh, University of		1,660*
	Washington	D.C.	525
	Pittsburgh	Pennsylvania	1,135
200	Northeastern		1,652*
	Boston	Massachusetts	1,652
203	Alaska, University of		1,614*
	College Village	Alaska	1,614
220	Arizona, University of		1,445
	Tucson	Arizona	1,445
221	Cincinnati, University of		1,429*
	Cincinnati	Ohio	991
	Dayton	Ohio	218
	Cornwells Heig	Pennsylvania	220
228	Analytic Service Inc		1,340*
	Falls Church	Virginia	1,340
230	Georgia Tech Research Institute		1,330*
	Eglin AFB	Florida	40
	Atlanta	Georgia	1,290
234	United States Commerce Department		1,298*
	Boulder	Colorado	600
	Denver	Colorado	75
	Washington	D.C.	582
	Gaithersburg	Maryland	16
	Rockville	Maryland	25
235	Smithsonian Institute		1,294*
	Washington	D.C.	1,197
	Cambridge	Massachusetts	97
238	Research Triangle Institute		1,282*
	Durham	NCAR	1,282
239	Washington University		1,281*
	St. Louis	Missouri	1,281
240	Syracuse University		1,279*
	Syracuse	New York	1,257

DEFENSE CONTRACTORS

NON-PROFIT INSTITUTIONS—Fiscal Year 1967 (*Cont'd.*)

RANK	NAME OF CONTRACTOR AND LOCATION		THOUSANDS OF DOLLARS
241	Texas A & M Research Foundation		1,257
	College Station	Texas	1,257
243	Illinois Institute of Technology		1,209*
	Chicago	Illinois	1,209
252	New Mexico, University of		1,144*
	Albuquerque	New Mexico	330
	Sandia	New Mexico	814
257	Yale University		1,101*
	New Haven	Connecticut	969
	Alamogordo	New Mexico	132
259	Southern California, University of		1,085*
	Los Angeles	California	1,085*
260	North Carolina, University of		1,080*
	Chapel Hill	NCAR	948
	Raleigh	NCAR	132
268	Oklahoma, University of		1,025*
	Fort Sill	Oklahoma	199
	Norman	Oklahoma	826
269	Lowell Tech Institute		1,024*
	Bedford	Massachusetts	73
	Billerica	Massachusetts	45
	Lowell	Massachusetts	906
275	Wentworth Institute		985*
	Bedford	Massachusetts	73
	Boston	Massachusetts	759
	Hamilton	Massachusetts	72
276	Lehigh University		985*
	Bethlehem	Pennsylvania	985
278	Travelers Research Center		980*
	Hartford	Connecticut	980
285	Florida, University of		912*
	Gainesville	Florida	912
286	Utah State University		907*
	Logan	Utah	907

DEFENSE CONTRACTORS

NON-PROFIT INSTITUTIONS—Fiscal Year 1967 (*Cont'd.*)

RANK	NAME OF CONTRACTOR AND LOCATION		THOUSANDS OF DOLLARS
288	Georgia Institute of Technology		902*
	Atlanta	Georgia	902
293	Stevens Institute of Technology		889*
	Bedford	Massachusetts	136
	Hoboken	New Jersey	753
296	Rhode Island, University of		877*
	Kingston	Rhode Island	877
298	Rice University		870*
	Houston	Texas	870
301	National Society Professional En		850*
	Washington	D.C.	850
307	Iowa State, University of		826*
	Iowa City	Iowa	826
310	New Mexico Institute Mining & TE		821*
	Socorro	New Mexico	821
315	Tennessee, University of		770*
	Knoxville	Tennessee	377
	Memphis	Tennessee	170
	Tullahoma	Tennessee	223
317	Oklahoma State, University of		758*
	Stillwater	Oklahoma	758
318	Hawaii, University of		756*
	Honolulu City	Hawaii	756
322	American Institute of Research		750*
	Palo Alto	California	80
	Washington	D.C.	139
	Silver Springs	Maryland	218
	Pittsburgh	Pennsylvania	313
327	Rochester, University of		734*
	Rochester	New York	734
329	Texas Western College		728*
	El Paso	Texas	728

DEFENSE CONTRACTORS

NON-PROFIT INSTITUTIONS—Fiscal Year 1967 *(Cont'd.)*

RANK	NAME OF CONTRACTOR AND LOCATION		THOUSANDS OF DOLLARS
333	Hudson Institute		713*
	Croton-on-Hudson	New York	548
	Hudson	New York	165
348	Ohio State University		658*
	Columbus	Ohio	658
351	Case Institute of Technology		654*
	Cleveland	Ohio	654
352	Lovelace Foundation		653*
	Albuquerque	New Mexico	653
357	Catholic University of America		633*
	Washington	D.C.	633
360	Boston College		626*
	Chestnut Hill	Massachusetts	384
	Weston	Massachusetts	242
361	Southern Research Institute		625*
	Birmingham	Alabama	625
362	Rensselaer Polytechnic Institute		621*
	Troy	New York	621
378	Missouri University		587*
	Columbia	Missouri	362
	Kansas City	Missouri	50
	Rolla	Missouri	175
379	Rutgers University		585*
	New Brunswick	New Jersey	585
380	Alabama, University of		583*
	Birmingham	Alabama	120
	Huntsville	Alabama	283
	University	Alabama	180
400	American Society for Engineering		539*
	Washington	D.C.	539
407	Arctic Institute of North America		532*
		Canada	60
		Greenland	95

DEFENSE CONTRACTORS

NON-PROFIT INSTITUTIONS—Fiscal Year 1967 (*Cont'd.*)

RANK	NAME OF CONTRACTOR AND LOCATION		THOUSANDS OF DOLLARS
	Washington	D.C.	377
409	Tufts University		528*
	Boston	Massachusetts	150
	Medford	Massachusetts	378
413	Michigan State University		514*
	East Lansing	Michigan	470
	Lansing	Michigan	15
	Rochester	Michigan	29
419	Notre Dame, University of		496*
	Notre Dame	Indiana	496
433	Western Reserve University		480*
	Cleveland	Ohio	480*
437	Kansas, University of		477*
	Kansas City	Kansas	76
	Lawrence	Kansas	401
442	Tulane University		464*
	Covington	Louisiana	190
	New Orleans	Louisiana	274
446	University Corp Atmospheric Research		460*
	Sunspot	New Mexico	460
449	Indiana University		449*
	Bloomington	Indiana	418
	Indianapolis	Indiana	31
453	New Hampshire, University of		440*
	Durham	New Hampshire	440
455	Flight Safety Foundation		437*
	Phoenix	Arizona	437
474	Washington State College		398*
	Alamogordo	New Mexico	63
	Pullman	Washington	335
489	Wayne State University		377*
	Detroit	Michigan	377

DEFENSE CONTRACTORS

NON-PROFIT INSTITUTIONS—Fiscal Year 1967 (*Cont'd.*)

RANK	NAME OF CONTRACTOR AND LOCATION		THOUSANDS OF DOLLARS
491	Louisiana State University of		375*
	Baton Rouge	Louisiana	326
	New Orleans	Louisiana	49
498	Saint Louis University		366*
	St. Louis	Missouri	366
499	United States H E W Department		365*
	Washington	D.C.	75
	Atlanta	Georgia	290
			655,160**

FOREIGN CONTRACTORS

90 E W R Fairchild International JV		5,900*
	Germany	
04 Canadian Commercial Corporation		4,872*
	Canada	4,872
08 Bristol Siddfley		825*
	United Kingdom	758
Edwards	California	67
26 Norway Minister of Defense		740*
	Norway	740
82 Mactaggart Scott & Company Ltd		386*
	United Kingdom	386
		12,723**

TOTAL FEDERAL OBLIGATIONS TO 100
LARGER AMOUNTS
(Dollar Amounts

INSTITUTION NAME	STATE	RANK	TOTAL FEDERAL OBLIGATION	AGRIC.
University of Michigan	Mich.	1	66,265	54
Mass. Inst. of Technology	Mass.	2	63,232	2
Stanford University	Cal.	3	60,621	0
Columbia University	N.Y.	4	60,041	12
University of Illinois	Ill.	5	58,491	4,255
Harvard University	Mass.	6	54,008	30
U. of Cal. Los Angeles	Cal.	7	51,298	50
U. of Cal. Berkeley	Cal.	8	50,315	4,212
University of Chicago	Ill.	9	45,286	1
Ohio State University	Ohio	10	39,025	4,520
University of Pennsylvania	Pa.	11	38,908	10
U. of Wis. Madison	Wisc.	12	38,756	3,669
University of Texas	Tex.	13	38,208	0
New York University	N.Y.	14	37,688	0
Pennsylvania State Univ.	Pa.	15	37,659	4,831
U. of Minn. Mnpls. St. Paul	Minn.	16	35,935	3,587
University of Washington	Wash.	17	35,575	136
Cornell University	N.Y.	18	35,324	3,924
Johns Hopkins University	Md.	19	31,994	1
Yale University	Conn.	20	29,830	44
Washington University	Mo.	21	27,265	0
University of Missouri	Mo.	22	26,644	3,891
Indiana University	Ind.	23	26,397	27
Purdue University	Ind.	24	26,157	3,988
University of Florida	Fla.	25	25,202	2,383
University of Pittsburgh	Pa.	26	24,873	156
University of N.C. at Chapel Hill	N.C.	27	24,591	0
Duke University	N.C.	28	23,693	11
University of Rochester	N.Y.	29	23,597	0
University of Maryland	Md.	30	23,425	1,626
University of Southern California	Cal.	31	22,718	0
Michigan State University	Mich.	32	22,369	4,187

UNIVERSITIES AND COLLEGES RECEIVING THE
BY AUGUST, 1966
in Thousands)

AEC	COMMERCE	DEPT. OF DEFENSE	HEALTH, ED. & WELFARE	INTERIOR	NASA	NATL. SCIENCE FOUNDATION
2,463	194	21,579	30,856	979	4,658	5,482
3,985	192	35,078	7,539	76	7,691	8,669
662	243	21,930	20,880	494	6,825	9,587
4,853	21	14,829	31,582	84	1,195	7,465
5,091	27	14,075	25,064	417	1,498	8,064
1,103	0	5,881	37,328	247	2,715	6,704
4,323	30	11,492	25,720	241	3,907	5,535
783	54	5,399	23,893	457	5,684	9,833
4,562	200	5,077	24,393	0	2,674	8,379
537	0	4,238	23,535	301	888	5,006
271	4	8,510	23,599	0	1,027	5,487
3,144	122	1,036	22,450	459	1,421	6,455
990	0	6,145	23,443	246	2,146	5,238
1,923	28	4,715	26,909	103	1,357	2,653
642	13	2,364	24,318	178	1,711	3,602
2,148	0	921	21,625	0	3,014	4,640
2,719	0	1,999	23,227	987	560	5,947
1,481	0	8,220	15,860	489	918	4,432
919	62	3,791	23,720	159	391	2,949
3,712	35	1,711	17,401	0	917	6,010
256	19	2,549	21,820	60	628	1,933
307	0	372	17,696	398	601	3,379
194	0	564	22,382	9	361	2,860
1,377	0	3,767	8,573	164	1,317	6,971
563	5	1,015	10,748	303	2,177	8,008
507	5	2,715	17,947	177	1,250	2,116
182	0	2,254	19,369	183	305	2,298
1,199	0	3,141	14,314	44	388	4,596
4,710	0	1,274	10,977	59	1,663	4,914
1,810	60	3,364	12,049	168	2,351	1,997
611	13	2,200	12,469	79	1,282	6,064
1,657	0	394	10,533	199	315	5,084

OBLIGATIONS BY THE DEPARTMENT OF
AT 100 UNIVERSITIES AND COLLEGES
(Dollar Amounts

INSTITUTION NAME	STATE	RANK	DEPT. OF DEFENSE
Mass. Inst. of Technology	Mass.	1	35,078
Stanford University	Cal.	2	21,930
University of Michigan	Mich.	3	21,579
Columbia University	N.Y.	4	14,829
University of Illinois	Ill.	5	14,075
U. of Cal. Los Angeles	Cal.	6	11,492
University of Pennsylvania	Pa.	7	8,510
Cornell University	N.Y.	8	8,220
University of Texas	Texas	9	6,145
Harvard University	Mass.	10	5,881
U. of Cal. Berkeley	Cal.	11	5,399
University of Denver	Colo.	12	5,307
University of Chicago	Ill.	13	5,077
Syracuse University	N.Y.	14	5,045
Brown University	R.I.	15	4,790
New York University	N.Y.	16	4,715
Northwestern University	Ill.	17	4,714
Ohio State University	Ohio	18	4,238
California Inst. of Tech.	Cal.	19	3,801
Johns Hopkins University	Md.	20	3,791
Purdue University	Ind.	21	3,767
University of Dayton	Ohio	22	3,641
Princeton University	N.J.	23	3,602
George Washington University	D.C.	24	3,433
University of Maryland	Md.	25	3,364
Duke University	N.C.	26	3,141
Carnegie Inst. Technology	Pa.	27	2,874
University of Pittsburgh	Pa.	28	2,715
Washington University	Md.	29	2,549
Polytechnic Inst. Brooklyn	N.Y.	30	2,487
Pennsylvania State University	Pa.	31	2,364
University of N.C. at Chapel Hill	N.C.	32	2,254

DEFENSE FOR RESEARCH AND DEVELOPMENT
RECEIVING THE LARGEST AMOUNTS, 1966
in Thousands)

ARMY	NAVY	AIR FORCE	DEFENSE AGENCY	DEPT.-WIDE FUNDS
5,485	9,672	17,542	2,379	0
5,951	8,174	5,126	2,679	0
10,868	1,560	7,314	1,837	0
1,138	8,935	4,756	0	0
6,419	2,391	3,141	2,071	53
1,348	9,337	807	0	0
4,276	802	932	2,500	0
2,785	838	2,198	2,376	23
669	4,214	1,262	0	0
2,109	1,445	1,035	1,292	0
1,055	2,380	1,676	253	35
424	163	4,696	24	0
1,937	488	1,487	1,165	0
1,269	3,066	710	0	0
1,984	614	544	1,648	0
1,765	1,451	1,499	0	0
1,769	869	258	1,818	0
360	180	3,523	0	175
789	2,075	937	0	0
1,450	910	1,381	0	50
1,544	474	804	945	0
0	50	3,591	0	0
843	1,857	885	17	0
358	3,042	33	0	0
2,140	250	399	536	39
2,672	145	324	0	0
1,754	947	173	0	0
1,574	443	620	0	78
1,381	20	148	1,000	0
153	1,323	1,011	0	0
967	509	868	0	20
1,222	110	288	634	0

UNIVERSITY OFFICIALS ON CORPORATE BOARDS

FORTUNE RANK	COMPANY	DIRECTOR WHO IS UNIVERSITY OFFICER	UNIVERSITY	SHARES
1	General Motors	James R. Killiam, Jr., Chairman of the Corporation	MIT	150
2	Ford Motor	Franklin D. Murphy, Chancellor	University of California	100
	"	Paul C. Cabot, Treasurer	Harvard	2,000
4	General Electric	Edwin D. Harrison, President	Georgia Institute of Technology	130
	"	Frederick L. Hovde, President	Purdue	10
6	Socony Mobil Oil	George P. Baker, Dean	Graduate School of Business Administration— Harvard	—
	"	Grayson L. Kirk, President	Columbia	640
7	Texaco, Inc.	Admiral Arleigh Burke, Director	Center for Strategic Studies—Georgetown University	1,400
9	I.B.M.	Grayson L. Kirk, President	Columbia	154
13	Swift & Co.	John A. Barr, Dean	Graduate School of Business Administration— Northwestern	200

	Swift & Co.	W. Allen Wallis, President	University of Rochester	100
17	Bethlehem Steel	Jess H. Davis, President	Stevens Institute of Technology	—
18	International Harvester	John T. Rettaliata, President	Illinois Institute of Technology	—
20	Radio Corporation of America	Lewis L. Strauss, President	Institute for Advanced Studies— Princeton	1,784
57	Litton Industries, Inc.	Myles L. Mace, Professor	Graduate School of Business Administration— Harvard University	17,304
58	Tenneco, Inc.	Earl Rudder, President	Texas A. & M. University	1,010
59	Ralston-Purina Co.	Dr. Earl L. Butz, Dean	School of Agriculture— Purdue University	620
66	McDonnell	George E. Pake, Provost & Professor of Physics	Washington University, St. Louis, Missouri	—
67	Grumman Aircraft Engineering Corp.	Ellis L. Phillips, Jr., Professor of Law	Columbia University	3,020
68	Inland Steel	Frederick L. Hovde, President	Purdue University	65
69	Bendix Corp.	Richard G. Folsom, President	Rensselaer Polytechnic Institute	200

UNIVERSITY OFFICIALS ON CORPORATE BOARDS (Cont'd.)

FORTUNE RANK	COMPANY	DIRECTOR WHO IS UNIVERSITY OFFICER	UNIVERSITY	SHARES
72	Corn Products, Inc.	Herbert E. Longenecker, President	Tulane University	100
73	Douglas Aircraft Co.	Dr. Willard F. Libby, Director	Institute of Geophysics & Planetary Physics— University of California, Los Angeles	—
75	B. F. Goodrich Co.	A. Kelly, Director	Purdue Research Foundation— University of Akron	14,000
		Deane W. Malott, President Emeritus	Cornell University	700
78	Jones & Laughlin Steel Corp.	J. C. Warner, President Emeritus	Carnegie Institute of Technology	424
84	Pittsburgh Plate Glass Co.	J. C. Warner, President Emeritus	"	200
85	Colgate-Palmolive Co.	William P. Tolley, Chancellor	Syracuse University	
87	Honeywell, Inc.	John J. Wilson, Secretary of the Corporation	MIT	57,919
88	Borg-Warner	George P. Shultz, Dean	Graduate School of Business— University of Chicago	100
90	Owen-Illinois	E. C. Arbuckle, Dean	Graduate School of Business— Stanford University	100
92	American Motors	William E. Stirton, Vice-President	University of Michigan & Director of Dearborn Campus, Ann Arbor	321
		Edward L. Cushman, Vice-President	Wayne State University	2,530
100	J. P. Stevens & Co., Inc.	Edwin D. Harrison, President	Georgia Institute of Technology	10

112	National Biscuit Co.	Jess H. Davis, President	Stevens Institute of Technology	200
113	Raytheon Co.	Harvey Brooks, Dean	Engineering & Applied Physics— Harvard University	100
120	Martin-Marietta Corp.	William A. Burns, Lecturer	Graduate School of Business— University of California	1,000
124	The Mead Corp.	Vernon R. Alden, President	Ohio University	100
145	Xerox	John Bardeen, Professor	Electrical Engineering & Applied Physics— University of Illinois	1,205
147	General Mills, Inc.	Deane W. Malott, President Emeritus	Cornell University	1,500
150	Hunt Foods & Industries	Roger W. Heyns, Chancellor	University of California	—
152	Philip Morris	Jess H. Davis, President	Stevens Institute of Technology	300
153	Quaker Oats	James H. Hilton, Director	University Development— Iowa State University	—
155	George A. Hormel & Co.	James C. Hormel, Assistant Dean & Dean of Students	University of Chicago Law School	—
180	Koppers Company, Inc.	Horton Guyford Stever, President	Carnegie Institute of Technology	200
184	Air Reduction Co., Inc.	Richard G. Folsom, President	Rensselaer Polytechnic Institute	—
187	American Machine & Foundry Co.	Frederick Seitz, Professor	Physics— University of Illinois	—
192	Dresser Industries	Robert S. Morse, Senior Lecturer	Sloan School of Management— MIT	—

UNIVERSITY OFFICIALS ON CORPORATE BOARDS (Cont'd.)

FORTUNE RANK	COMPANY	DIRECTOR WHO IS UNIVERSITY OFFICER	UNIVERSITY	SHARES
193	Carrier Corp.	Jess H. Davis, President	Stevens Institute of Technology	150
	Carrier Corp.	Albert W. Snoke, Executive Director	Yale New Haven Hospital	300
197	Foremost Dairies Inc.	Dr. Robert R. Dockson, Dean	School of Business Administration—University of Southern California	200

MERCHANDISING FIRMS

FORTUNE RANK	COMPANY	DIRECTOR WHO IS UNIVERSITY OFFICER	UNIVERSITY	SHARES
1	Sears, Roebuck	J. Roscoe Miller, President	Northwestern	1,100
2	Great Atlantic Pacific Tea	None	Graduate School of Business—Stanford	100
3	Safeway Stores	Ernest C. Arbuckle, Dean		
4	Kroger	W. George Pinnell, Dean	Graduate School of Business—Indiana	100
5	J. C. Penney	None		—
6	Montgomery Ward	None		—
7	F. W. Woolworth	None		—
8	Federated Department Stores	Howard Wesley Johnson, President	MIT	117
9	Acme Markets	Willis J. Winn, Dean	Wharton School of Finance & Commerce	—
10	Food Fair Stores	None		

UTILITIES

FORTUNE RANK	COMPANY	DIRECTOR WHO IS UNIVERSITY OFFICER	UNIVERSITY	SHARES
1	American Tel. & Tel.	James R. Killian, Jr. Chairman of the Corporation	MIT	594
2	Consolidated Edison	Grayson L. Kirk, President	Columbia	232

3	Pacific Gas & Electric	*None*		
4	Commonwealth Edison	John A. Barr, Dean	School of Business—Northwestern	243
5	Southern California Edison	*None*		
6	Southern Co.	*None*		
7	American Electric Power	Courtney C. Brown, Dean	Graduate School of Business—Columbia	1,538
8	Public Service Electric & Gas	Richard C. Folsom, President	Rensselaer Polytechnic Institute	100
9	Columbia Gas System	Jess H. Davis, President	Stevens Institute of Technology	
10	El Paso Natural Gas	John C. Baker, President Emeritus	Ohio University	1,266

Transportation Companies

1	Pennsylvania R.R.	Gaylord P. Harnwell, President	University of Pennsylvania	1,500
2	Southern Pacific	*None*		
3	United Air Lines	*None*		
4	Pan American World Airways	*None*		
5	Chesapeake & Ohio R.R.	*None*		
6	New York Central R.R.	*None*		
7	Atcheson, Topeka & Santa Fe	John T. Rettaliata, President	Illinois Institute of Technology	100 preferred 100 common
8	American Airlines	Courtland Davis Perkins, Chairman	Department of Aerospace & Mechanical Sciences—Princeton	

UNIVERSITY OFFICIALS ON CORPORATE BOARDS *(Cont'd.)*

FORTUNE RANK	COMPANY	DIRECTOR WHO IS UNIVERSITY OFFICER	UNIVERSITY	SHARES
9	Trans World Airlines	*None*		—
10	Union Pacific R.R.	Courtney C. Brown, Dean	School of Business— Columbia	—

TOP TEN LIFE INSURANCE COMPANIES

FORTUNE RANK	COMPANY	DIRECTOR WHO IS UNIVERSITY OFFICER	UNIVERSITY	SHARES
1	Prudential Insurance Company of America	Jess H. Davis, President	Stevens Institute of Technology	—
	"	John E. Deitrick, Dean	Cornell University Medical College	—
	"	James M. Hester, President	New York University	—
2	Metropolitan Life Insurance Co.	*None*		—
3	Equitable Life Assurance Society of the U. S.	Robert F. Goheen, President	Princeton	—
		Francis C. Wood, Professor	Medical University of Pennsylvania	—
4	New York Life Insurance	Katherine E. McBride, President	Bryn Mawr College	—
5	John Hancock Mutual Life Insurance Co.	George F. Bennett, Treasurer Howard Johnson, President	Harvard MIT	—
6	Aetna Life Insurance	John Perry Miller, Dean	Graduate School— Yale	—
	"	Ernest C. Arbuckle, Dean	Graduate School of Business— Stanford University	—

7	Northwestern Mutual Life Insurance Co.	None	—	
8	The Travelers Insurance Co.	None	—	
9	Connecticut General Life Insurance Co.	Dr. Albert C. Jacobs, President	Trinity College, Hartford, Conn.	
10	Massachusetts Mutual	None	Wesleyan	—

Notes

THE MACHINE

The quotation from Paul Weiss comes from *Right & Wrong*, by Paul Weiss and Jonathan Weiss (page 24). "Notes on the Post Industrial State (I)," by Daniel Bell was published in the winter, 1967, issue of *Public Interest* (page 30). Statistics on education vary widely, but the following sources are useful: *Projections of Educational Statistics to 1974–75* and *Digest of Educational Statistics, 1967* (both are published by the Office of Education in the Department of Health, Education and Welfare). Also see *Federal Funds for Research, Development and other Scientific Activities* by the National Science Foundation. *The Politics of Pure Science*, by Daniel S. Greenberg, describes how the scientists got involved with the government. *The Uses of the University*, by Clark Kerr, gives a short history of the government's growing involvement with education over the years. In *The New Industrial State*, John Kenneth Galbraith discusses the importance of educators in the society.

THE DIRECTORS

For more information on spin-offs around Cambridge, see "Technology Transfer and Entrepreneurial Success," a paper presented at the 1966 Conference on the Administration of Research by Edward B. Roberts and Herbert A. Wainer, both of the Sloan School at MIT. Roberts and several of his students have been looking into this subject in detail and there are other papers available. The suit involving Northwestern University is on file in the clerk's office for Cook

County in Chicago. The entanglements between university officials in Michigan and outside business interests have received a good bit of play in the newspapers over the past couple of years. For a summary of the situation see the editorial page of the *Wall Street Journal,* December 5, 1967. Also, opinion No. 4492 by Frank J. Kelley, attorney general of Michigan, March 10, 1966; and Kelley's opinion No. 4587 of September 26, 1967.

THE UNIVERSITY BUSINESS

For the details on Harvard's interest in Middle South Utilities, see the company's 1966 proxy statement. Details of Yale's investment scheme are set forth in the Treasurer's Report for 1967, and in the registration statement for Omega Fund, Incorporated, which was filed with the Securities and Exchange Commission. The public portions of the income tax returns for WARF may be examined at the Internal Revenue Service, and they provide some clue as to the business of the organization. In February, 1967, the President's Science Advisory Committee published a report called "Computers in Higher Education." Another useful document is "Digital Computer Needs in Universities and Colleges." It was put out in 1966 by the National Academy of Science. The "1966 Progress Report on Western Data Processing Center," published by UCLA, gives the details of that operation. The quote from R. W. Gerard comes from a speech he made entitled "Computers and Education" before the Fall Joint Computer Conference in December, 1965.

THE PROPRIETORS

See the annual reports of Abt Associates and Simulmatics, as well as the registration statement for a public offering of Simulmatics stock on file with the Securities and Exchange Commission. Donald A. Schon's book *Technology and Change* offers an interesting discussion of his theories on the form of the corporation. The quote is from page 135. Sterling Livingston's comics are distributed by the Labor Department.

POLITICS

The quotation from Theodore H. White concerning action

intellectuals comes from an article in the June 9, 1967, issue of *Life,* entitled "In the Halls of Power." Wright Patman's comments on the use of law reviews is from the *Congressional Record,* August 25, 1957, pages 16159-69. Justice Douglas' speech is entitled "Law Reviews and Full Disclosure," and was printed in the *Washington Law Review,* June, 1965. Morton Mintz' book *By Prescription Only* provides a fuller description of the activities of Dr. Cass. Dr. Kligman discussed the inaccuracies in his researches in a letter to the *Journal of the American Medical Association,* September 26, 1966, page 161. The two Richardson-Merrell memos were introduced as evidence in the trial of Ostopowitz *v.* Richardson Merrell. The case was tried in the White Plains Supreme Court during the fall of 1966. Telegrams from the various university officials were read on the Senate floor and published in the *Congressional Record,* June 28, 1965, pages 14396-415. For a fuller description of the Rostow and Markham testimony before the Senate Antitrust and Monopoly Subcommittee, see Part 4 of the hearings on S1552, December, 1961, beginning at page 2044. The text of Dr. Gilman's letter was inserted into the *Congressional Record* (page S12840) by Senator Hugh Scott on September 12, 1967. For details on Casavan Industries, see the registration statement filed with the Securities and Exchange Commission, and the record of Casavina's trial. He was tried in the spring of 1965 by jury in federal district court in Newark, N. J. Cornell University's role in suppressing information on traffic safety was discussed during hearings before both the Senate Subcommittee on Executive Reorganization (*Traffic Safety,* Part 2, July, 1965, beginning at page 682) and the Senate Commerce Committee. See the hearings on S3005, March-April, 1966, page 346.

WAR

Some of the most informative reporting on the universities' relationships with the military is contained in the little-known papers and magazines which have sprung up on the left. *New Left Notes,* which is put out by Students for a Democratic Society in Chicago, often carries items of interest in this area. There is an excellent and detailed description of both Stanford University's and the Stanford Research Institute's involvement with the military by David Ransom in the March 9 and April 4, 1967, issues of *Resistance*. The winter, 1967, issue of *Viet Report* contains a run-down on university relations with the Pentagon. It includes a long piece on IDA, a guide to help one plow through the federal indexes in order to discover military research contracts and a list of gas contracts. Elinor Langer was among the first to get into the gas business, and her articles appeared during the winter of 1966 in *Science*. Seymour Hersh's book *Chemical and Biological Warfare* gives a detailed account of gas research at universities. The House Appropriations Committee hearings are an excellent source of material on this subject. In the spring of 1968 the Senate Foreign Relations Committee published hearings on the Defense Department's foreign affairs research. They were held May 9, 1968. Most of the CIA material comes from reporting, carried out in part by the author at the *New Republic*. The material was published in the magazine in a lead editorial March 4, 1967. The House Subcommittee on International Organizations and Movements ran hearings on Project Camelot January 25, 1966. The various reports of HumRRO and CRESS can be obtained through the Commerce Department's Clearinghouse for Federal Scientific and Technical Information. On page 677 of *The Code Breakers*, David Kahn makes clear the purpose of Princeton's communications center.

MULTIVERSITY, INC.

The students at Berkeley published two interesting monographs describing the power of the Regents and their relations to economic interests in the state. One is called "The Regents," by Marvin Garson and Ken Blum. It is published by the Independent Socialist Club, P.O. Box 910, Berkeley 1, California. The other is "Big Business and the American University," by Bettina Aptheker, and it can be obtained from New Outlook Publishers in New York. Some of the incidents described in this chapter are also discussed in these monographs. Paul S. Taylor has written voluminously about land and water use in California. See "On Reclamation Law," in *The American West*, March, 1968. The magazine is published by the Western History Association. See *Resistance*, March 9 and April 4, 1967 issues, for more on Stanford.

URB-COIN

The *Politics of Urban Renewal*, by Rossi and Dentler, has a history of urban renewal as it affects the Hyde Park neighborhood of Chicago. Real estate transactions involving Columbia are recorded at the Hall of Records in Manhattan; for Long Island University, at Borough Hall in Brooklyn or at Riverhead, Long Island, the county seat of Suffolk County. Assemblyman Joseph Kottler, chairman of the Joint Legislative Committee on Higher Education, conducted hearings on the proposed sale of LIU during the fall and winter of 1967. A good deal of interesting material is revealed in these.

Index

Suitt, William, 95
Sulzberger, Arthur Ochs, 97, 98
Suppes, Patrick, 50
Swibel, Charles, 156-57
Symonds, Gardner, 152

Tax exemption, 186, 195
Teledyne, 39
Teller, Edward, 4, 112
Temple, Allen H., 181
Tenneco, 152
Texas, University of, 14, 39-40, 100
Textile Research Institute, 16
Thai-American Steel Works, Company, 152
Thermal Dynamics, 14
Thomas, Charles S., 144-45
Thomas, David, 95
Thor, Eric, 149-50
Time magazine, 45, 46, 65
Time Share Corporation, 14
Times-Mirror Company, 19, 22, 142
Tobacco industry, 89-105
Tobacco Industry Research Committee, 91
Tobacco Reporter, 92
Tobacco Research Council, 93-94
Torr, Donald, 65
Tracor, Inc., 14
Training Development Center, 64
Transportation Association of America, 73
Tregoe, Benjamin B., 108
Tribus, Myron, 51-52
Truman, David, 175
Truman, Harry S., 139
Tschirgi, Robert, 47-48
Tukey, John, 75, 134-35
Tulane University, 131
Tuma, Elias H., 150

Udall, Stewart, 142
Umberger, Charles, 95
Underhill, Robert, 141, 145
University City Science Center, 41
University Microfilms, 28-29
University officials on corporate boards, 18-23
Unruh, Jesse, 139
Urb-Coin Game, 58, 156-92
Uris, Percy, 180-81
Uris Buildings Corporation, 180-82
Utah Construction and Mining Company, 151, 153, 154

Vandenburg Construction Company, 32
Van Fleet, General James, 187
Vietnam war, 71, 113, 115-16, 119, 123, 125-26, 129, 154
Volkswagen, 109

Wagner, Robert, 189
Wainer, Herbert A., 13
Wall Street Journal, 12, 102-103
Walton, Clarence C., 175, 176
Washington University, 78, 84-85
Watkins-Johnson Company, 152
Watson, Thomas J., Jr., 24, 25, 41
Watts, John C., 93
Wayne State University, 92, 94
Webb & Knapp, 187
Weekly Reader, 9
Weisner, Jerome, 25
Weiss, Paul, 1
Wellman, Harry, 148
Wells-Fargo Bank, 151
Werner, Howard W., 81
Wescoe, W. Clarke, 28
Wesleyan University, 9

Psychotherapy
East & West
Alan W. Watts

Eternity is *Now*—and in this major book Alan
Watts explores the ways of liberation developed
by East and West: liberation from repression
of the body and emotions, liberation from the
prison of the ego, liberation from the meaning-
less routines of consumption and production
that our civilization has imposed on mankind.
By the author of *The Book: On the Taboo
Against Knowing Who You Are.*

A BALLANTINE BOOK $.95